CONTENTS

Master Key Series (Prosperity)	3
Introduction	4
Here Is How You Can Use This Book Efficiently	5
Copy and Paste	6
Do not over Repeat	7
Tell It to People Around	8
AFFIRMATIONS	9

MASTER KEY SERIES (PROSPERITY)

New 2000 Positive Affirmations to aid Your Self-Confidence

John Goldberg

All rights reserved. No part of this book may be reproduced or transmitted in any form or by any means, electronic or mechanical, including photocopying, recording, or by any information storage and retrieval system, without permission from the author. Brief excerpts may be cited in book reviews, provided the narrative quoted is verbatim and due credit is given by way of the book title and name of author

INTRODUCTION

It is getting harder for people to motivate themselves these days. And we need to positively motivate ourselves at every critical point of our lives. There are so many things that are intent on crushing your passion and stopping you from reaching all the long and short-term goals you have set for yourself.

Well, even if the year 2019 has seemingly passed without you getting to hit those targets, the next year will not pass you by! This is the reason why these new 2000 positive affirmations are important for you to master. When you look through them, you would be immediately struck by how much effort I put into curating it for you. Have these in mind:

- The Positive Affirmations will aid you in your quest to build your brand effectively
- The Positive Affirmations will help you go through that painstaking Weight-loss program that you have always been avoiding
- These Positive Affirmations will aid you in sticking to your spiritual journey even when you feel like falling off.

I could tell you a hundred more benefits of these positive affirmations but I want you to delving into them yourself.

HERE IS HOW YOU CAN USE THIS BOOK EFFICIENTLY

COPY AND PASTE

Don't only recite the Positive Affirmations just like others that you have. Take a further step by copying them and pasting them to strategic areas in your home. It doesn't matter if it is on the fridge, T.V, Door that you choose to paste them. Just make sure they are in a place that you can easily see them. By doing this, you are invariably forcing them into your subconscious- which is where they should be!

DO NOT OVER REPEAT

I know that this advice seems a bit off, but I want you try it. The usual advice that you hear is that you should keep repeating Positive Affirmations for many times. Well, what happens when you do that is that it can easily turn into a chore and will become boring. Rather than mentioning the same line for ten times in an hour, try for only four times. Then, see the magic.

TELL IT TO PEOPLE AROUND

I have discovered that this is one of the most dynamic ways to improve your mastery of Positive Affirmations. Personalize the Positive Affirmations for your friends, family, co-workers, and every other person. The next effect of this is that you will find it easy to commit the declarations to memory AND THEY WILL HELP SPUR YOU.

Enough with all these talk; let's move straight into the positive declarations.

AFFIRMATIONS

1. It will be well with me because I am on the right track
2. I know I can, and I will learn how to successfully manage my appetites
3. I know I can, and I will learn how to be efficient in my character
4. I know I can, and I will learn the means to rightly correct my character flaws
5. I know I can, and I will learn how not to be a mood killer
6. I know I can, and I will learn how to correctly comport myself in all situations
7. I know I can, and I will learn how to properly covey my thoughts without issues
8. I know I can, and I will learn how to disagree without being disagreeable
9. I know I can, and I will learn how to channel my anger rightly
10. I know I can, and I will learn how to read the meanings behind people's actions so I do not jump easily into conclusions.
11. I know I can, and I will learn how to remain focused even within the midst of a terrible storm that

threatens to distract and overwhelm me

12. I know I can, and I will learn how to efficiently ride through the eye of the storm
13. I know I can, and I will learn how to gradually forgive others for the wrongs they have done to me because I may be of service to them in the future
14. I know I can, and I will learn how not to hold on to past hurt and groom bitterness in my heart
15. I know I can, and I will learn how to move on from past disappointment so that new doors of favor can be opened in its stead
16. I know I can, and I will learn how to pick up the broken pieces of my past, mold them together, and start glowing because my journey is still very much on course
17. I know I can, and I will learn the billionaire state of mind so that I can adapt mine to it
18. I know I can, and I will learn the billionaire work schedule so that I can reconfigure my to fit in
19. I know I can, and I will learn the billionaire reading culture so that I can open my mind to receiving the same set of instructions that made them become who they are
20. I know I can, and I will learn the billionaire manner of speech so that I do not hold on to the same set of speeches that has kept me down
21. I know I can, and I will learn what it means to properly court success
22. I know I can, and I will learn how Billionaires identify little opportunities and their investment patterns

Master Key Series (Prosperity)

23. I know I can, and I will learn how Billionaires like Jeff Bezos, Bill Gates, Warren Buffet etc. rose to the top of their industries with sheer force of willpower and determination

24. I know I can, and I will learn how visionary minds like Steve Jobs, Mark Zukerberg, and others overcame early jitters in their journey to owning global conglomerates

25. I know I can, and I will learn how countries like United Arab Emirates and Singapore were able to organize their little resources to build amazing cities within short period of time

26. Since I know that education is key towards gaining prosperity, I will learn how to properly utilise education to groom my confidence

27. Since I recognize the fact that failure does not bring many friends, I will stay in my loneliness and keep on working on myself and products until they become the best

28. Since I recognize the fact that success brings so many people who will be new friends, I will never forget those who stood by me from the first day I started

29. Since I recognize the fact that success always attracts many sycophants, I will ensure that I still keep my true friends that can critisze me around

30. Since I recognize the fact that proper education can help someone to retain a sense of dignity, I will always chase after knowledge

31. Since I know that a single mistake can cause years of effort to be lost, I will ensure that I always remain on guard

32. Since I know that every action of a successful person

is always being scrutinized, I will try and ensure that I do not become overly complex

33. Since I understand that I am the one that holds my destiny in my hands, I will not be lax in doing what needs to be done at the time it needs to be done

34. Since I recognize that I have the power to control my emotions, I will always keep a lid on them and will not be caught slipping

35. Since I recognize that loyalty pays, I will be disciplined enough and loyal to my mentors so they can show me the right path to tread and the ones to refrain from

36. Since I understand the being different brings the attraction most times, I will strive to bring a different approach in many of my dealings

37. Since I understand that Fortune 500 companies like dynamic problem solvers, I will rise to the occasion by always provide actual strategies that will work within special situations.

38. Since I understand that success will take its toll on my body and mind, I will ensure that they are both kept in great shape at all times.

39. Since I understand that people love smart dressers, I will strive to always dress exquisitely well so that I would be given special recognition

40. Since I realize that most people are usually given one shot to hit the target and become successful, I will make sure I am fully prepared for that day when I will be called on to take that one short

41. Since I recognize that practice is the activity that makes perfection, I will strive never to miss one single day of practice

42. Since I recognize the fact that my coaches know better than me, I will be humble enough to listen to them before arguing back
43. Since I recognize that golden trophies are won at the back of blood stained sweat, I will be willing to put in that amazing effort to make it there
44. Since I realize that money should not be my ultimate motivator, I will ensure that I prioritize value creation and career progression more than money
45. Since I realize the fact that I can peak at any time in my industry, I will always scout around for new challenges that would keep me fresh and focused
46. Since I recognize that people who fail are always complaining, I would not be one of such people
47. Since I recognize that successful people are willing to spend big to get comfort and peaceful state of mind, I will not mind the cost when it comes to getting peace of mind
48. Since I recognize the fact that successful people are good at getting out of their comfort zone to do the 'dirty work', I will not be the person that becomes too comfortable to leave the comfort zone

49. It is well with me as I go out today
50. I know I can, I know it is within my range of goals, and I will not falter nor stop
51. everything will keep working out for my good as long as I stay focused on this part of success
52. it will be well with me and my family today, tomorrow and the entire length of this year

53. as long as I live I will pursue success
54. I live success
55. I breed success
56. I do everything with success
57. there is no stopping my flow of creativity
58. there is no stopping my flow of brilliance t
59. here is no stopping my flow of excellent thoughts
60. there is no stopping my flow of uniqueness
61. I am going to reach the top no matter what my peers say or believe
62. I am going to surprise everybody by making it to the top of my career
63. I live prosperity
64. I do not only aspire to become prosperous, I know I will become prosperous with the right mentality and the right set of coaching I will be prosperous
65. I can choose the best coaches in the world
66. I do not have to settle for less when choosing my coach
67. I have the best set of friends around me to push me to achieving my purpose in life
68. I am walking in excellence freedom to achieve all God has for me
69. It doesn't matter if I am bruised battered and shattered by the waves of many disappointments I will still reach the top of my game
70. I know I can, I know it is within my range of goals, and I will prosper

Master Key Series (Prosperity)

71. I know I can, I know it is within my range of goals, and I will succeed despite a few of the numerous roadblocks of pain that is set before me

72. I know that I have the seed of prosperity blossoming inside me

73. it doesn't matter if I am not seeing the evidence now, I will still believe that I am the best

74. I believe I am a king in my area of expertise

75. I believe as I walk, I am walking into excellence

76. I am ready to achieve any of the good things that I have set for myself in my goals

77. I know I can, I know it is within my range of goals, and I will not procrastinate in this journey of reaching my goal

78. I know I can, I know it is within my range of goals, and I will not be set back by my wilful laziness

79. I know I can, I know it is within my range of goals, and I will be totally disciplined towards achieving everything that I have set out to achieve

80. I am setting goals that will help me achieve every good thing in life

81. I am going to work by the goals that I have set for myself in reaching the goal and set destination that I love in life

82. My short-term goals are going to lead me to the good destination of life

83. My long-term goals are pure unique and will be effective if I put my mind to it

84. It does not matter the mental distractions that come to my mind, I will still stay strong on this

course of achieving my goals

85. I am a custodian of excellence
86. I am a custodian of brilliant ideas
87. I am a custodian of many ground-breaking inventions
88. I know I can, I know it is within my range of goals, and I will put these ideas into practice and achieve the best results that I could ever have
89. I know I can, I know it is within my range of goals, and I will put these inventions into motion and keep on refining them till they become the ideas I have in my head
90. I bring the party with me wherever I go
91. I am a legendary *networker*
92. I move with purpose and do not look around those who are purposeless
93. I know I can, I know it is within my range of goals, and I will not sit by and watch my destiny go unattended to
94. I know I can, I know it is within my range of goals, and I will chip in daily efforts and pray that God will bring excellence to the Mix
95. I know there is a throne waiting for me and I will reach that throne room and be applauded
96. I know there is a counsellor that can lead me on the right path
97. I know I can, I know it is within my range of goals, and I will keep looking for that counsellor and will cherish every counsel
98. I know I can, I know it is within my range of goals,

and I will not be proud to the extent that I fail to recognise the importance ideas of everybody around me

99. I know I can, I know it is within my range of goals, and I will not be proud to the extent that I refuse to learn on a daily basis

100. I know I can, I know it is within my range of goals, and I will not be proud to the extent that I keep my ideas to myself and steal other people's ideas

101. I know I can, I know it is within my range of goals, and I will work my ass off to ensure that my ideas pay and I will not be afraid to throw away ideas just because I am emotionally attached to them

102. I know I can, I know it is within my range of goals, and I will never be so emotionally attached to a single cause of action that I fail to see a better one

103. I know I can, I know it is within my range of goals, and I will move and step in the part of happiness on a daily basis

104. when I start my morning, it will be with positive thoughts

105. when my afternoon comes, I will not allow the negativity of the morning take control and when the evening comes I will take stock of everything that happened in the day

106. I know I can, I know it is within my range of goals, and I will not be a person that lives a very disorganised life

107. I would rather live a very organised with

my plans and goals

108. a closed mind never reaches anywhere; that is why I will always ensure that my mind remains open

109. I know I can, I know it is within my range of goals, and I will learn from everything

110. I know I can, I know it is within my range of goals, and I will learn from every words that people speak

111. I know I can, I know it is within my range of goals, and I will learn from every actions that people take

112. I know I can, I know it is within my range of goals, and I will learn from every inaction that people do not take

113. I know I can, I know it is within my range of goals, and I will learn from every facial gesture that people do

114. I know I can, I know it is within my range of goals, and I will learn by giving to people

115. I know I can, I know it is within my range of goals, and I will give out value to people so that I can get value back

116. I know I can, I know it is within my range of goals, and I will not be someone that always takes and keeps on taking without giving anything back

117. I know I can, I know it is within my range of goals, and I will not be a closed system that refuses to open up

118. Rather I will be an open system that al-

lows things to flow through

119. I know I can, I know it is within my range of goals, and I will not be rude and saucy to people I meet today

120. I know I can, I know it is within my range of goals, and I will always guard my tongue from bursting out in anger

121. Prosperous people are always watchful of the steps they take and I will always be watchful of every step that I take

122. I know I can, I know it is within my range of goals, and I will not be put inside boxes

123. I know I can, I know it is within my range of goals, and I will not be confined by what society defines as success

124. I know I can, I know it is within my range of goals, and I will break the norm and become extravagantly successful

125. I know I can, I know it is within my range of goals, and I will not be held on a leash of ideas

126. I know I can, I know it is within my range of goals, and I will allow my ideas to roam and brought forth into reality

127. I know I can, I know it is within my range of goals, and I will get a dynamic team that will help me to reach my desired destination

128. My dynamic team will consist of people who will not be afraid to say the truth at all times

129. My dynamic team will consist of people who will not be afraid to tell me opposite ideas

130. My dynamic team will consist of people

who are not necessarily going to share my single ideas but will be willing enough to listen to me

131. My dynamic team will be made up of people who are goal oriented

132. My dynamic team will be made up of people who are always going for gold

133. My dynamic team will be made up of people who believe in themselves despite their failures

134. My dynamic team will be made up of Fighters who will always rise above every down periods

135. My dynamic team will be made of people who will not be afraid of integrating new ideas into practice

136. My dynamic team will be made up of people who can cook up unique inventions

137. My dynamic theme will be made up of people who sound intellectual and back up their words with their right action

138. My dynamic team will not necessarily be my fans rather they will be people who are of integrity

139. I know I can, I know it is within my range of goals, and I will be someone that remains honest in the face of every shade of corruption

140. I possess the ability to recycle old stuff and make it unique

141. I possess the ability to rebrand myself and make myself better

142. I know I can, I know it is within my range

of goals, and I will strive to be in the presence of people who are better than me

143. I know I can, I know it is within my range of goals, and I will strive to avoid the presence of people who are going to stop me from reaching the top

144. I know I can, I know it is within my range of goals, and I will strive to pay for the value that will take me to the top

145. I know I can, I know it is within my range of goals, and I will not rely on free things all the time

146. Rather, I will be someone that is willing to pay the price of discipline and hard work

147. I know I can, I know it is within my range of goals, and I will not be afraid to use technology to achieve my purpose

148. I know I can, I know it is within my range of goals, and I will not remain stuck in the past because of my fear of the future

149. I know I can, I know it is within my range of goals, and I will not remain stagnated because of my fear of what I need to do to move ahead

150. I know I can, I know it is within my range of goals, and I will mentally train myself to improve my ability to change

151. I know I can, I know it is within my range of goals, and I will be adaptable and flexible at all times

152. I know I can, I know it is within my range of goals, and I will not be strong headed and maintain my wrong positions if it is going to stop me

from reaching the top

153. I know I can, I know it is within my range of goals, and I will have the patience to be thorough in everything I do

154. I know I can, I know it is within my range of goals, and I will have the patience to function

155. I know I can, I know it is within my range of goals, and I will have the ability to run every large corporation

156. I know I can, I know it is within my range of goals, and I will develop the key skills to succeed in every craft

157. I know I can, I know it is within my range of goals, and I will develop the mental strenght to combat the rigors of managing people

158. I know I can, I know it is within my range of goals, and I will not shy away from speaking the truth to everyone

159. I know I can, I know it is within my range of goals, and I will not shy away from speaking the bitter truth to myself

160. When I catch myself slipping off, I will not be that person that keeps on doing it

161. Rather, I will develop a means to caution myself and start doing right

162. I know I can, I know it is within my range of goals, and I am going to get a mentor that I will be accountable to

163. I know I can, I know it is within my range of goals, and I am going to get a mentor that will teach me the tricks of rising up after falling

164. I know I can, I know it is within my range of goals, and I am going to get a mentor that will teach me the tricks of moving upward in my craft

165. I know I can, I know it is within my range of goals, and I am going to get a mentor that will always find a way to correct me thoroughly and helping me to rise again

166. I know I can, I know it is within my range of goals, and I am going to get a mentor that will not be afraid to look me in the eye and say the raw truth

167. I know I can, I know it is within my range of goals, and I am going to get a mentor that may not be the most popular but has gone ahead in the field that I currently find myself

168. I know I can, I know it is within my range of goals, and I am going to get a mentor that knows how to effectively teach me negotiating skills

169. I know I can, I know it is within my range of goals, and I am going to get a mentor that will teach me how to maintain a steady course of optimal efficiency

170. I know I can, I know it is within my range of goals, and I am going to get a mentor that will teach me how to develop core communication skills that is even better than what I currently have

171. I know I can, I know it is within my range of goals, and I am going to get a mentor that Will show me the ropes on managing my career decisions

172. I know I can, I know it is within my range of goals, and I am going to get a mentor that will

teach me how to manage social relationships within every sphere of life that I find myself

173. I know I can, I know it is within my range of goals, and I am going to get a mentor that will teach me how to walk and talk among CEOs and also introduce me to the culture of those who are prosperous

174. I know I can, I know it is within my range of goals, and I am going to get a mentor that will ensure that my time is well patterned so that every moment of the day is effective

175. I know I can, I know it is within my range of goals, and I am going to get a mentor that will teach me the value of rest and play so that I will not work myself to an early grave

176. I know I can, I know it is within my range of goals, and I am going to get a mentor that will help me understand some nuances about leadership so that I do not end up being consumed by its rigors

177. I know I can, I know it is within my range of goals, and I am going to get a mentor that will teach me what it takes to build other people like me and the key features to spot in a potential leader

178. I know I can, I know it is within my range of goals, and I am going to get a mentor that will help to console me when I need a shoulder to cry on because I know that the journey into prosperity will lead me on a thorny path

179. I know I can, I know it is within my range of goals, and I am going to get a mentor that will be quick to show me the good turns on the path of

prosperity and help me avoid the mistakes that other people have made

180. I know I can, I know it is within my range of goals, and I am going to get a mentor that will help me to avoid falling into the shortcuts that will ruin me just like it has ruined others

181. I know I can, I know it is within my range of goals, and I am going to get a mentor that will ensure that I refrain from every act of foolishness that may potentially tarnish my image and spoil all the good works I have started

182. I know I can, I know it is within my range of goals, and I am going to get a mentor that will recognise the importance of saying the right words at the right time so that I am positively encouraged

183. I know I can, I know it is within my range of goals, and I am going to get a mentor that will never be eventually jealous of my success but will be willing to celebrate with me on the grandest stage

184. I know I can, I know it is within my range of goals, and I am going to get a mentor that can teach me how to remain motivated even if I seem to have reached the top of my field

185. I know I can, I know it is within my range of goals, and I am going to get a mentor that will open my eyes to the need to give out myself, time, and resources to charity so that I can make the world a better place

186. I know I can, I know it is within my range of goals, and I am going to get a mentor that will teach me how to avoid reacting to everything the way normal people would do

187. Rather, the mentor would teach me how to properly respond after giving it a quick thought

188. I know I can, I know it is within my range of goals, and I am going to get a mentor that will teach me the most important instinctive skills to have so that it would be a natural part of me

189. I know I can, I know it is within my range of goals, and I am going to get a mentor that will teach me the most important communication skills that will help me resolve every escalating situation on my way to the top

190. I know I can, I know it is within my range of goals, and I am going to get a mentor that will teach me the most important people management skills so that I will be able to harmonize a group towards achieving the goals that we have

191. I know I can, I know it is within my range of goals, and I am going to get a mentor that will teach me the most important life lessons that the person got from a time of the person's life

192. I know I can, I know it is within my range of goals, and I am going to get a mentor that will teach me the most important set of steps to take when I first enter a new position in my career

193. I know I can, I know it is within my range of goals, and I am going to get a mentor that will teach me the most important lesson tips when I want to choose my friends and romantic relationships

194. I know I can, I know it is within my range of goals, and I am going to get a mentor that can point me towards a true religious experience that will give me inner peace even as I am seeking for

physical riches

195. I know I can, I know it is within my range of goals, and I am going to get a mentor that can show me the importance of abstaining from certain practices that I may think has been good all along the way

196. I know I can, I know it is within my range of goals, and I am going to get a mentor that can pour time and pool resources into me because the mentor believes that I have what it takes to succeed

197.

198. I know I can, I know it is within my range of goals, and I will always ensure that I furnish and complete every little detail of the work I engage in

199. I know I can, I know it is within my range of goals, and I will always present the best content for my clients

200. I know I can, I know it is within my range of goals, and I Will develop my Unique Selling Point and ensure that it is dynamic and different from other competitors'

201. I know I can, I know it is within my range of goals, and I will develop the unique pitch that will get the job done at all times

202. I believe that I have what it takes to match my competitors product for product

203. I believe that I have what it takes to deliver the best service for every of my clients

204. I believe that I have what it takes to make my product resonate deeply within the conscious-

ness of my buyers

205. I believe that I have what it takes to make my service become more acceptable by my audience

206. I believe that I have what it takes to make my talent become shown to the entire world

207. I believe that I have what it takes to develop my skills and ensure that it is not a copycat of other professionals

208. I believe that I have what it takes to make my brand adopt a brilliant glow that makes it irresistible to other clients

209. I believe that I have what it takes to break into new markets and solidify my product's hold there

210. I believe that I have what it takes to make my clients and other people refer me to new clients

211. I believe that I have what it takes to start learning a skill that I think is very difficult

212. I believe that I have what it takes to start being strategic with the life moves I am taking as regards to being prosperous

213. I believe that I have what it takes to guide the people in my team towards achieving their own levels of greatness

214. I believe that I have what it takes to succeed in an environment even if many people have complained bitterly and left suddenly

215. I believe that I have what it takes to make the elements work together in my favor and also create the best peaceful environment

216.   I believe that I have what it takes to fight off the numerous wild animals of pain, pressure, and disappointment that are waiting behind after dark to finish me off

217.   I believe that I have what it takes to fight off the vultures in my industry who are circling around and waiting for my dream to die off

218.   I believe that I have what it takes to make it even if I have been deserted by the people and companies that people regard as the best

219.   I believe that I have what it takes to find my way to the green fields of opportunity and reap the good things of life

220.   I have what it takes to overtake my competitors

221.   I know I can, I know it is within my range of goals, and I will always look out for the best opportunities to better serve my clients

222.   I know I can, I know it is within my range of goals, and I will always reach out to meet my clients even if they are not reaching out

223.   It does not matter how long it will take for me to make my name go viral, I will still continue to put in the necessary efforts to bring it

224.   it doesn't matter how long it may take for me so overcome depression, I will overcome this and become prosperous again

225.   It doesn't matter what the financial experts are saying, I will still be at the top

226.   it doesn't matter the economy forecasts of experts at this time, I will still make headway

227. I will not foreclose my home due to economic downturns

228. I know I can, I know it is within my range of goals, and I will not lose out on life

229. Even if I lose out on life I will not stay down because there is a better position waiting for me

230. I know I can, I know it is within my range of goals, and I will always be calm in the face of storms

231. I know I can, I know it is within my range of goals, and I will develop the core principles needed for life

232. I know I can, and I will develop the core principles of emotional intelligence so that I will always be in charge of my emotions.

233. I know I can, and I will develop core character principles of financial intelligence

234. I know I can, and I will be financially disciplined enough to push through my goals of life

235. I know I can, and I will be financially disciplined enough to attain prosperity like never before

236. I know I can, I know it is within my range of goals, and I will read up books that teach on prosperity and ensure I put their principles into daily practice

237. I know I can, I know it is within my range of goals, and I will learn the benefits of time management on this pursuit of becoming excellent

238. I know I can, I know it is within my range of

goals, and I will learn how to engage in goal setting

239. I know I can, I know it is within my range of goals, and I will learn how to adequately engage in time chunking

240. I know I can, I know it is within my range of goals, and I will be an excellent delegator

241. I know I can, I know it is within my range of goals, and I will always ensure that I dedicate some activities to some of the members of my team

242. I know I can, I know it is within my range of goals, and I will be willing enough to trust my team members with key positions

243. I know I can, I know it is within my range of goals, and I will not be a paranoid person

244. I know I can, I know it is within my range of goals, and I will not be a paranoid leader

245. I know I can, I know it is within my range of goals, and I will not be a paranoid lover

246. I will not be a paranoid friend

247. Because paranoia does not bringing excellence I will never be paranoid

248. I have foresight to become a prosperous person

249. I am blessed with the skills to manage people and take them to the top

250. I am blessed with the skills to forecast rightly and I will ensure I reach the top

251. I know I can, I know it is within my range of goals, and I will guard my heart against negative

self limiting thoughts

252. I know I can, I know it is within my range of goals, and I will guard my heart against the words of people who do not believe themselves

253. I know I can, I know it is within my range of goals, and I will guard my heart against any form of Pride that may want to bring me down

254. I know I can, I know it is within my range of goals, and I will always look out for opportunities where I can see them

255. I know the rules of the game and will continue to learn more and more about them

256. I know I can, I know it is within my range of goals, and I will utilise these rules of the game of life and make the best out of it

257. I am a great manager and I will always believe in myself

258. I may not have a large circle of Friends but I will ensure that that circle consist of people who are like-minded and understand the value of time

259. Even though this industry seems to be scary, I will still overcome because I have the seed of greatness in me

260. I know I can, I know it is within my range of goals, and I will always have boundaries for people so they don't destroy my efforts

261. I know I can, I know it is within my range of goals, and I will reward myself when there is an opportunity to do so and I will celebrate every little victory that I get

262. However I will not always rely on past

victories

263. Rather I will move ahead and become better

264. I know I can, I know it is within my range of goals, and I will learn the value of thanking people for whatever thing they do for me

265. I know I can, I know it is within my range of goals, and I will learn the value off discussing my ideas with people

266. I know I can, I know it is within my range of goals, and I will not place too much pressure on people so they don't break down

267. Rather I will not them towards helping them achieve their dreams and I will become more prosperous because of that

268. I know I can, I know it is within my range of goals, and I will ensure that everything is top notch and my brand is recognised for excellence

269. Since prosperity entails health as well I will enjoy the best health ever

270. I know I can, I know it is within my range of goals, and I will ensure that I do everything to keep up health regime

271. I know I can, I know it is within my range of goals, and I will ensure I prepare unique tasteful recipes to keep my health up

272. I know I can, I know it is within my range of goals, and I will read up health books to help me keep fit

273. I know I can, I know it is within my range of goals, and I will not allow my body to be a de-

posit for junk because my health is wealth

274. I know I can, I know it is within my range of goals, and I will ensure I keep on monitoring my health levels

275. I know I can, I know it is within my range of goals, and I will pay attention to what my dietitian and doctors say about my health

276. I know I can, I know it is within my range of goals, and I will go for the necessary checkups to ensure that I detect anything early

277. I know I can, I know it is within my range of goals, and I will maintain a good morning health regime

278. I am in a unique position to make a great move today

279. I am going to step into the shoes of greatness today

280. I am a shot-caller that calls the shots of unique decisions

281. I am at liberty to delete every negative thought of poverty in my life

282. I am the manager of my life and I will always move on from terrible stages

283. I am being called by God into a great position in life.

284. I know I can, I know it is within my range of goals, and I will move ahead from the pain of past disappointments

285. I know I can, I know it is within my range of goals, and I will move ahead from the traps that I set for myself in the past

286.   I know I can, I know it is within my range of goals, and I will not go back act in denial today by choosing not to meet my challenges

287.   I know I can, I know it is within my range of goals, and I will face my challenges head-on with the knowledge that I have greatness in me

288.   I know I can, I know it is within my range of goals, and I will unearthen that seed of mediocrity in me and crush it totally

289.   I know I can, I know it is within my range of goals, and I will scale from the helicopter of fear and jump into the wind of opportunity.

290.   I know I can, I know it is within my range of goals, and I will stare down the face of failure and tell it to go away!

291.

292.   As I move in this journey of life things will work out fine for me

293.   prosperity is the standard I live by

294.   Prosperity is the air I breathe in

295.   I am a living, breathing testimony that will outshine my expectations

296.   In terms of expectations, I would exceed everything

297.   I am working according to explicit instructions for prosperity

298.   I am moving according to the dictates of my passion and I will reach the top

299.   Many are the distressing signals for me to

stop but I won't listen to them

300. Many are the calls for me to give up at this early stage but I will not be a part of such

301. Prosperity has many friends and I am a very close friend as well

302. I know I can, I know it is within my range of goals, and I will not settle for what others define as the best. I would rather strive to my last breathe to reach all my goals

303. I know I can, I know it is within my range of goals, and I will not be a party to those who compromise their standards.

304. I know I can, I know it is within my range of goals, and I will be a model example for legally earned prosperity

305. I am soaring higher than I have ever been put down by recent issues but they are only setbacks meant to push me toward becoming the best

306. I am not the person I was by yesterday

307. I have matured in the wisdom to handle issues better and reach prosperity faster

308. There would be no incidence of giving up while I am on this watch

309. Though I may fall down two times in this quest to become prosperous, I will rise two thousand times

310. Though there are some distractions that may wish to take my eyes off the prize, I will remain focused

311. I know I can, I know it is within my range of goals, and Like the giraffe, I will stand tall above

every negative things that may wish to derail me

312. I know I can, I know it is within my range of goals, and I will achieve maximum speed in the attainment of purpose

313. Just like Oprah, I know I can, I know it is within my range of goals, and I will create an empire that would rival other empires in the world

314. Just like Oprah, I know I can, I know it is within my range of goals, and I will remain a strong woman that beats the odds in my pursuit of success

315. Just like my favorite football player (put the name here), I will keep on scoring

316. As I am running toward the top, my eyes will always remain on the prize

317. It does not matter the injuries that beset me, I will still rise to continue in this game of life

318. Prosperity will remain drawn toward my businesses

319. Prosperity will remain a unique friend that I will eat and dine with daily

320. I am crossing the bridge of determination into the other side of prosperity soon

321. I am moving into the territory of success today

322. I speak my prosperous day into life this moment.

323. I know I can, I know it is within my range of goals, and I will enjoy the total benefits of the pain of determination

324. Today is a crowing day of each and every

effort I have put into reaching the top

325. I am emotionally ready for success

326. I know I can, I know it is within my range of goals, and I will not panic when faced with the prospect of success

327. I know I can, I know it is within my range of goals, and I will not break down in fear when an opening of success presents itself

328. I know I can, I know it is within my range of goals, and I will be emotionally ready to handle the challenges that the new stage of success will bring my way

329. I know I can, I know it is within my range of goals, and I will be ready to work on every element of laziness that would want me to slow down once I am successful

330. I know I can reorganize my relationships to fit into my journey to success

331. I know I can pick the kind of friends I want that will inspire me to success

332. I know I can provide the best kind of value that will help my friends to reach their best potentials

333. I know I have some qualities that can attract the kind of prosperity I want

334. I know I have the strength to cut off negative relationships that are not pushing me towards success

335. I do not have to remain in a hurtful friendship if it is affecting my ability to be successful

336. I am worthy of being given good attention

and motivated towards success

337. I am not going to be used and dumped in any relationship because it may stop me from being successful

338. I know that my romantic relationship will work toward the goal of prosperity.

339. I attract good things my way as I move around today

340. Everything is working out for my good because I deserve it

341. I know I can, I know it is within my range of goals, and I will not be a failure in wherever area I find myself.

342. It does not matter where ever I turn, I would always meet favour from people

343. I know I can, I know it is within my range of goals, and I will attract good people to me today and repel every negative person that brings bad energy towards me

344. I received all the good things that God has in store for me

345. It does not matter who comes my way, I will always try to ensure that I leave them better than I met them

346. I know I can, I know it is within my range of goals, and I will operate in the realm of love today and reach out to touch lives in a positive way today

347. It does not matter what my mind tells me about my self-esteem, I know deep down in my heart that I am unique

348. It does not matter how much my mind thinks that I do not deserve good things, I know in my heart that I should get the best that today has to offer.

349. It does not matter how far I have come close to breakthrough, I will hit it this time

350. It does not matter how twisted and windy the path of success is, I will still reach the destination with glee

351. It does not matter how many thousand kilometer that the destination of success is, I will still reach it

352. Because President Benjamin Franklin succeeded due to force of sheer will, I will succeed

353. Just like Captain Conel Sanders succeeded through force of sheer passion, I will succeed through my passion

354. Just like President Obama became a president in the midst of great uncertainties, I will reach the top despite every uncertainty that life throws my way

355. Just like Usain Bolt reached the top of his potential and still remained on top for long, I will reach the top of my game and remain there for long

356. Just like Margaret Thatcher reached the top of the British political sphere despite her gender, I will overcome every gender barrier that aims to stop me from reaching the top

357. Just like Chimamanda Adichie became one of the best authors in literature, I will challenge those narratives that have pitched me to fail

358.   It does not matter if I do not find it easy in climbing the steps into victory, I will still reach that top

359.   It does not matter if those at the top have spent decades there, I will still reach the place and dominate

360.   It does not matter how long my name has been omitted from the scoreboard, I will still be celebrated

361.   It does not matter how long my head has been bowed due to lack of applause, I will soon lift up my head to acknowledge every good applause that will come my

Affirmation of Specialness

362.   I have the gene of success coded into my genes

363.   I have the hands of a winner and will keep on making hits wherever I go

364.   I have the eyes of a champion and will keep seeing opportunities where others see stumbling blocks

365.   I have eyes like the eagle and will keep on seeing clearly despite the storms of life that may come my way

366.   I have the strength of an eagle and will keep flying through the eye of every storm that attempts to bring me down

367. I have the strength of an eagle and I will snap up every opportunity that comes my way.

368. There would be no opportunity too difficult for my eyes to miss at every point in time

369. I have the roar of a lion and will always get what I want when I show up

370. It does not matter how bad things I, I will still remain at the top of the food chain because I have the blood of a winner running in my veins

371. Like the lion of the jungle, I will never cower in the presence of any challenges that I am faced with

372. Like the lion and his territory, I will keep on reigning in this territory of mine and nothing will put me off

373. I know I can, I know it is within my range of goals, and I refuse to believe that my weakness is better than me

374. I know I can, I know it is within my range of goals, and I refuse to believe that I cannot scale through any height

375. I know I can, I know it is within my range of goals, and I refuse to believe that I am not made for better things

376. I know I can, I know it is within my range of goals, and I refuse to believe that I am not worth more than a million

377. I continue to believe that I am indispensable to my organization

378. I continue to affirm that I am indispensable to my family

Master Key Series (Prosperity)

379. I continue to believe that I am meant for better things.

380. Just like the elephant, I am big, strong and bold enough.

381. Just like the elephant in stride, I cannot be stopped when I am in motion

382. Just like the cheetah, I will be quick to spot the good things of life

383. I know I can, I know it is within my range of goals, and I will be the best I can be

384. All things are working together for my good

385. I know I can, I know it is within my range of goals, and I will always Excel whenever I find myself

386. If there is anywhere success is, I will be there.

387. Everything will fall into the right places for me today wherever I go

388. I know I can, I know it is within my range of goals, and I will encounter massive success and favor my family will enjoy me

389. I am a living breathing testimony

390. I am working on the path of greatness

391. Wherever I Go, greatness follows

392. Whatever I will do greatness comes from it

393. Whatever I say greatness is in it

394. There is no stopping me from reaching every goal and objective I have set for myself

395. There is no stopping me from meeting the best people that life has to give to me

396. There is no stopping me from wearing the quotes of favour wherever I go

397. When I look at the stars I see myself there

398. When I look at the sun I see myself shining brightly all the days of my life

399. When I think about my future I smile because things will go fine

400. When I think about the past I smile because I have learnt lessons for the future

401. Whenever I think about evil things I remember that God is there to push me to greater Heights

402. It doesn't matter who says or whatever says I am not great if I believe I will be become great in everything I do

403. I recognise that God can make it much more better

404. As I stare at this reflection of myself in the mirror I know I am looking at a great person

405. As I proceed to tender this contract I know I will get it

406. As I proceed to tender this contract I know things will fall in right places for me

407. As I proceed to tender this contract I know I have the confidence to speak and get people to buy into it

408. As I proceed to tender this contract I know I can, I know it is within my range of goals, and I will scale through

409. As I perceive to tender this contract I recognize this seed of greatness in me

410. As I proceed to tender this contract I recognise that I will be successful despite my weaknesses

411. I work with boldness

412. I walk in strength

413. I work in power

414. I walk in Liberty

415. I am walking daily in the love of god

416. Understand this I will be great

417. Understand this I will be the best I can be

418. Just like all the great people on earth I will take the pain that comes with greatness

419. Just like all the great people on earth I will live and bear the seeds of greatness.

420. Just like every other great person on Earth I will always work with the understanding that I am a king

421. Just like every other great person on Earth I will always work with the understanding that I am a queen

422. I am a king of this Kingdom in life

423. I am a king in this career

424. I have chosen to be great

425. Listen up, you have no excuse to fail

426. Listen up, you have no excuse to stop pursuing your dreams

427. Listen up, I have no excuse to be downcast at all times

428. Listen up, I have no excuse to keep on being put down by people

429. Listen up, I have no excuse to keep on remaining poor

430. Even though it takes me a long time, I know I can, I know it is within my range of goals, and I will still get it up

431. Even though it takes a long time, I know I can, I know it is within my range of goals, and I will still dying with champions

432. Even though it takes me a long time, I know I can, I know it is within my range of goals, and I will still shake hands with the best people in my craft

433. Even though it takes me a long time, I know I can, I know it is within my range of goals, and I will still be famous for what I love doing best

434. Even though it takes me a long time, this passion of mine shall pay off

435. Even though it takes me a long time, I know I can, I know it is within my range of goals, and I will still remain focused on the track of greatness

436. Listen to this, you are not a mediocre

437. Listen to this, you are not meant to keep on remaining a fool

438. Even though people may have hurt me in

the past, I know I can, I know it is within my range of goals, and I will still flourish in joy

439. I know I can, I know it is within my range of goals, and I will still enjoy the full happiness that life gives to me

440. I am healthy

441. I am beautiful

442. I am wise

443. I can do amazing things

444. I am worthy

445. I am balanced

446. I am motivated

447. I have the power that I need to succeed, I am powerful

448. I am powerful and present in my own life

449. I more than enough

450. I am special

451. I am the creator of my own life, I build its foundation and choose its content

452. I am calm and relaxed in any circumstances

453. I am filled with energy and exude happiness

454. I am indestructible

455. I radiate beauty, charm and grace

456. I feel great in my own skin

457. I feel great in my own body

458.   I trust myself to create a fantastic life
459.   I am ambitious
460.   I am a goal-getter and a risk-taker
461.   I am a diligent person
462.   I am valuable
463.   I don't wallow in self-pity
464.   I am beautiful and wonderfully made
465.   I am free to be myself
466.   I can do everything I set my mind to do
467.   I am positive and elegant

468.

469.   I am potent
470.   My body cells and tissue function well
471.   I am in a balanced state of health
472.   I am in love with my body and shape
473.   I have a beautiful body shape
474.   My body is healthy
475.   I eat healthily
476.   My body is in alignment with what I feel and think
477.   My behavior is aligned with my balanced state of mind
478.   I am blessed with sound health
479.   I love my body and respect it
480.   I am comfortable looking in the mirror and saying I love you, and I really love

481. I am elegant

482. I am beautiful in and out

483. Wellness is the natural state of my body

484. I am in perfect health

485. I am perfect just the way I am

486. I am whole and complete

487. Excellent health is my divine light, and I claim it now

488. I accept myself the way I am, and I love me

489. I am deeply in love with myself

490. I enjoy my own company, and I feel great being alone

491. I take care of everything that I own, my spirit, my body and my mind

492. I am always surrounded by health and vitality

493. My mind is brilliant

494. My soul is at peace

495. Fear is just a feeling, I overcome it, and I move forward

496. I am ready for any challenges

497. I am brave

498. I face any problem with courage

499. I am competent

500. I choose to be free from all fears and destructive thoughts

501. I am in charge

502. I meet my fears with power and courage
503. I am brave enough to live my dreams
504. I overcome fears by following my dreams
505. I am reliable and disciplined.
506. I am fearless and strong
507. In the eye of the storm, I remain calm
508. I cast out all my fears and accept change
509. I choose to breathe, trust, and let go
510. I am growing outside of my comfort zone
511. Nothing will stand in my way.
512. I will overcome any challenges.
513. I look forward to facing challenges as opportunities to grow.
514. I am so resilient and strong
515. I have faced challenges before and overcome them
516. It is in the brokenness that I am healing
517. I am climbing onward and upward
518. My mind is sharp, I can do anything

519. I will not stop the flow of Hustle
520. I will not stop because I was disappointed
521. My disappointment was very painful but I will rise again
522. I felt bad for being put down, but I will still continue to rise
523. It doesn't matter how many times I encountered disappointment, it will not stop me

Master Key Series (Prosperity)

from Rising

524. People may have taken my money and run away, but I will not wallow in depression
525. I will not be depressed because people did not believe in my art
526. It won't be long before my art pays

527. I will not continue eating out of this plate of pain
528. I will not allow the disappointment of a past client to stop me from moving ahead
529. I will not procrastinate because I have been bruised by past clients
530. I feel pained by someone trying to scam me but I will not stop providing value
531. I will not focus on the monies lost; instead I will focus on the value I am going to create more
532. I will not focus on the money is lost because I will take the experience is needed
533. It does not matter how many times I have been burnt by past clients, I will still rise and push my hustle to the top
534. I felt this pain deeply when the client stole my money but I will not stop
535. I will still continue to believe in myself and my craft
536. Even if the things around me are not encouraging, I will push myself out of this

537. I am in a city of Hustlers so I can't afford to be lazy
538. I am in a city of go-getters so I can't afford to rest
539. Every night I sleep I remain focused on my

51

hustle
540. Every night I sleep, I wake up as a giant ready for the day
541. I know I will succeed even though things do not seem too well

542. I will be encouraged by friends who stand by me
543. I will be in close contact to my family who supports me when my business is down
544. I will learn to support family when they are down
545. I will learn to allow people encourage me
546. When my business is going down I will remain teachable so people can help me achieve my dreams
547. On God I will survive in this business
548. I will always look out for treasures in this sea of opportunities
549. I will always dive in deep to identify opportunities wherever I find myself
550. I will charge the price that is befitting for my status
551. I will not dance with the Stars prematurely
552. My hustle and peace will not be shattered by cancellations
553. I will always ensure that my demand is high
554. Daily, I will look for ways to always meet up with my demand
555. I will not give excuses when fulfilling orders
556. I will not give half-baked responses to my

clients
557. I will not allow myself to be judged based on my past
558. I will strive to make my present much better
559. I will forecast excellent goals for my company

560. I will not neglect my boss duties
561. I will not allow procrastination to hinder me from functioning as a good leader
562. My team members will get the best of me at every point in time
563. I will always maintain a positive outlook when people see me
564. I will be a person of action
565. I will be a person driven by passion and make excellent impact
566. I will allow discipline to become my best friend to beat procrastination
567. I will develop the best health regimes ever to ensure that I function optimally
568. I will make every day count even if I work from home
569. I will still function optimally
570. I will create the environment that pushes me to function the best
571. I will declutter my environment to ensure I do not procrastinate
572. My environment will remain clean enough so I can maintain a positive frame of mind
573. I will enjoy the benefits of nature to inspire me in my business
574. I will take walks when it is necessary to boost my efficiency

575. It doesn't matter what mental challenge looms ahead for me I will be inspired to succeed

576. My heart is large enough to accommodate my passion
577. My mind is large enough to accommodate my vision
578. My hands are strong enough to work out my goal
579. My mouth is large enough to hunger for excellence
580. My teeth is strong enough to bite down pain
581. My ears are open enough to listen to discipline
582. My legs are strong enough to go to great places
583. My arms are long enough to take on new challenges
584. My nose is sensitive enough to smell out new opportunities
585. I will honour every invitation that will bring success to me
586. I really want my team members to succeed richly
587. I will be a dynamic team member that celebrates with my team
588. I will ensure I provide optimum contributions wherever society I find myself
589. I will not allow my vulnerable moments outshine me
590. I am designed to be perfect
591. Quick delivery will become my new motto
592. I will work in silence and provide max-

imum value

593. I will not be known as a regular sulker

594. My bag of potentials is filled and I will take every opportunity to showcase them
595. I will not carry negative baggage to where I go
596. I will not keep my potential is hidden from the world
597. Stability will be my watch word
598. Moderation will be my watch word
599. Vigilance is important and I will be vigilant over my business
600. Before the end of the year, I will achieve my dreams
601. Before year end, I would take care of procrastination
602. Before year end, my team will celebrate greatly
603. There is nothing like too late for me in achieving my dreams
604. Procrastination shall not be my daily words
605. I will look sharp and achieving my freaks
606. Appearance is key at all times and I will ensure my appearance is great

607. When problems arise I will not run away
608. When problems arise I will be there standing strong
609. I have willpower to develop extra-ordinary competence to handle issues
610. I will not be known as an abusive person

611. People will not refer to me as psychotic
612. Desperation will not be one of my key features
613. Despite the mistakes I make, I will not be a perpetual failure
614. I will develop key Concepts to help me succeed
615. Peer rejection will not stop me from reaching the top
616. I will handle peer rejections in stride
617. Peer rejections will not inspire me to procrastinate
618. I will not be preoccupied with fear of failure
619. Criticisms will only mold me in reaching the top
620. I will not neglect the essentials of business
621. There are many teachings on reaching the top I will get them and learn them
622. I will not put faith in friends alone
623. Since research is important, I will provide well designed research for my business

624. I will be committed in my business drafting
625. Out of basic needs of my business, I will create unique daily goals
626. Meticulousness is a character I will adopt
627. I will not be overly restrictive of ideas
628. My team members will find it easy to pitch ideas to me
629. Though I fall I will rise 10000 times
630. Though my business is not attracting media attention, I will not stop
631. Even if my business attracts negative at-

tention, I will not stop
632. It is Never Over Until My Mind determines it is over
633. There are many people who have risen out of the ashes, I will become one of them
634. There are many people who have risen out of obscurity, I will not die away
635. I will not unduly nag my coworkers in their pursuit of Hustle
636. Some people feel guilty of their success, I will not be one of them
637. I put in my strength and passion to have reached the top and I will not feel guilty about that
638. I will not procrastinate because I was abandoned by some business partners
639. This phase is just meant for me to learn and learn
640. I will develop great remedies that will make me bounce back
641. When people tell me of my procrastination, I will recognise it early
642. I will not block my ears to the honest criticisms from friends around
643. When people tell me about problems in my business model, I will listen to them
644. I will work on them to ensure that they become better
645. The most influential people are those that put in work daily
646. I will be influential because of the pure dedication I will give to my work
647. The most influential people are those who manage their procrastination
648. I will be influential because I will stop the excesses of procrastination
649. I will always be inspired to end my streak

of procrastination
650. When I sit, I will think success in my Hustle
651. When I walk, I will think greatness about myself
652. When I lie down, I will mentally calculate how I will increase my pay
653. When I rise up, I will be energized to get opportunities rolling
654. Repetition is the key to excellence in hustle
655. I will repeat the good principles I have learnt on a daily basis
656. I will repeat the principles adopted by successful people in my industry
657. I will not allow pride to cover my success

658. I will not allow tiredness to cover my hustle

659. Knowledge is Not Enough; I will back it up with strength
660. Listening to motivational speeches Is not Enough; I will back it up with swift action
661. Reading action books on goals Is Not Enough; I will back it up with clearly defined action plans I
662. will love my Hustle because it is the only thing available for me
663. I will put my soul into my Hustle because it's the only thing that drives me
664. My strength will not be wasted on needless pursuits
665. My behavior will be modeled by an excellent spirit

666. I will hustle until I leave long lasting legacies for my grandchildren
667. I will be careful in attending to my client's desires
668. The road to becoming accomplished is a bit difficult but I will follow that road

669. I will rear successful people like me

670. Since success can be multiplied, I will ensure I multiply successful people
671. Till we reach the top, I will not give needless comments on irrelevant things
672. Taking notes will be one of my important hobbies to reach the top
673. I need encouragement from my past successes
674. I will receive encouragement from my inner circle of influence
675. I will not needlessly provoke my team members to leave
676. Provocation will not be a character that my clients know me for
677. Bitterness will not be a trait my team members know me for
678. I will not be bitter because of past experiences
679. I will not allow bitterness drive me to procrastination

680. I will not withhold happiness from my team members because of their non-performance
681. I will not withhold happiness from myself because I did not reach expectations

682. I will not force my team members to accept my goals ideas
683. I will not force my coach to accept my goals and ideas
684. Admitting of my mistakes will be one of my key strengths
685. My clients will know me for admitting my wrongs quickly
686. My clients will know me for my penchant for improving my work

687. Everything I do lead to prosperity.
688. I live in abundance because my path drops fatness.
689. No matter the circumstances I find myself in I prosper beyond measures.
690. Mediocrity is not an option in my life, I am prosperous in all my dealings.
691. Prosperity is my portion and I have it.
692. I defer the odds surrounding my life and I move beyond the average into prosperity.
693. All of God's creation and creatures are compelled to work in favor and launch me in the realms of prosperity.
694. I will always get what I need because the universe delivers what I need to be prosperous.
695. I am prosperous in my thinking, my life rejuvenate prosperity.
696. My life attracts all round prosperity, I refuse to be small.
697. I let go of my mediocre mentality and prosperity is attracted to me naturally.
698. I am prosperous in spirit soul and body.

699. My mind is open to the wealth of prosperous ventures in the world, I live in abundance.
700. My life exhumes success, abundance and prosperity.
701. I am not at a disadvantaged level because abundance flows freely in me, it might not look like it now, I persuaded beyond any form of doubt that I am prosperous.
702. In life I break protocols and thread the path of prosperity against all inclination.
703. My life is an avalanche of abundance, I am a lender and not borrower.
704. I don't live at the mercy of men or circumstances, I live on my own terms.
705. Adversity has no effect on me, my life is a citadel of prosperity.
706. My life is reformed, my mind is reconstructed to greatness, I don't think small, so I cannot be small.
707. Prosperity suits me, I radiate abundance, I blossom and flourish.
708. I speak prosperity into existence in my life, I cannot die small, I refuse to be small.
709. Am in control of my life, I create prosperity, because the key to prosperity is in me.
710. I am the blessed of the Lord, I prosper in all ways.
711. Am very hopeful, things are getting better than it used to be, I just can't give up now because am assured beyond imagination that prosperity will suit me well.
712. I will take the required steps, that lead me closer to my goals, I won't give up until I walk into prosperity.
713. I won't allow my detractors make me give up, I will harness all opportunities until I attain

success in life.

714. I am capable of being prosperous, because prosperity is wired into my DNA.

715. I am focus, my past failures and mistakes can't hold me bound, I gravitate towards a prosperous life.

716. I pursue my dreams with reckless abandon, nothing and no one will stop me.

717. I am insurmountable, I am an embodiment of creative abilities, and failure don't have a grip on me.

718. I am a being of inestimable value, I deserve the best of the best in life, and they gravitate towards me.

719. I am unstoppable, I pursue my goals with all tenacity, and distractors are inconsequential.

720. I am productive in all circumstances, I achieve greatness in all my endeavors.

721. I am free from the fears that has held me bound for so long, I have been imputed with a sound mind because of this I am free to access prosperity and be prosperous in all my ways and dealings.

722. Things are working for my good, I'm scared of challenges, they are stepping stones to my upliftment.

723. I am a delightsome land I elicit, abundance, greatness and prosperity.

724. In hard times and paths, I stride on the pathway of greatness and prosperity, deterring fear of the unknown.

725. I have authority, things obey me, I am prosperous beyond my imaginations.

726. No matter the economic situation of my nation, I produce wealth effortlessly.

727. I am an abundance being, I breathe and

live in abundance no matter what is going on around me.

728. I have a strong faith in myself, nothing can stop me on my journey to success.

729. I am well positioned and I flourish in my season.

730. I am an embodiment of wisdom, I will always make the right decision towards prosperity.

731. I receive clarity of purpose, life happenings can't throw me off balance, I stay on the path of greatness till it manifests.

732. I receive clarity of purpose, people and circumstances can't toss me about, I pursue prosperity with all vigor.

733. I refuse to wallow in self-pity, I strive for success despite my past mistakes, lost and wasted opportunities.

734. Nothing and no one can stop my rising, I attain great heights in life and destiny.

735. I am full of grace and glory, I can't be relegated to the background.

736. My life is an overflow of blessings, I am a compartment of value, I add values to the people and beyond through my prosperity.

737. The works of my hands are bless, everything I torch prosper.

738. Everything around me might be screaming impossibilities, I am determined against all odds, that I am prosperous.

739. I move beyond all obstacle and I achieve major achievements in life that launches me into prosperity.

740. I am an epitome of greatness, I experience prosperity beyond measures.

741. I move from obscurity to limelight.

742. When face with issues that make men give

up, I refuse to concede defeat, instead I mount up with wings and soar above the obstacles.

743. I accomplish greater exploit, no matter how fierce the challenge may be.

744. I am the best of my kind, I operate a high frequency of prosperity.

745. I see clearly even in the storms of life, I can't be misguided by insightful assurance of my prosperous future.

746. I confront my challenges with all boldness, I refuse to be crippled by fear.

747. My life is an embodiment of all it takes for me to be successful.

748. I harness the wealth of opportunities around me to achieve greatness.

749. I scale through challenges with ease.

750. I see abundance, success, greatness and prosperity ahead of me.

751. I prosper in health and my mental wellbeing.

752. I embrace unlimited wealth into my life.

753. I am grateful for the successes I have recorded have, as I continue to stride the path of success.

754. I express abundance, success and greatness with my giftings and talents.

755. I surround myself with people who are capable contributing to my prosperity.

756. I consciously reproduce the lifestyle of success I want to live daily.

757. My actions and associations gravitate towards success, greatness, and prosperity.

758. I silence every thoughts and feelings of lack and incompetence and release my creative abilities to succeed.

759. I refuse to embrace laziness, I chose to pay

Master Key Series (Prosperity)

the price for success, until I prosper.

760. I am destined to succeed, circumstances can't change this.

761. My need are constantly met, as I follow the path of excellence, greatness and success.

762. I surmount all obstacles to my success and prosperity.

763. My thoughts are agreeable to God's prosperous plan for me.

764. Every day of my life I become more prosperous and successful despite the challenges that abound.

765. I unleash the power to succeed in me, I see success, greatness and prosperity.

766. I commit myself to a constant and never ending improvement in all that lead to my prosperity.

767. I transcend beyond my limiting belief of prosperity and become a better version of me.

768. I embrace change, learn new perspectives of life from other people's thinking and experiences.

769. I nurture my success and greatness with passion and enthusiasm.

770. I say no to the good, so that I can embrace the great, I leave my comfort zone.

771. I accelerate my prosperity, by learning from the perspectives, knowledge, experience and resources of successful people.

772. I make a commitment to broaden my horizon to succeed, no matter how tasking it might be.

773. I continually move forward towards the completion of my goals and achieving my dreams.

774. I commit to develop my intuition and trust my feelings, people won't dictate my life for

me, I am in charge.

775. I follow my inner guidance in making successful decision, concerning matters that affect my life.

776. I will not leave my prosperity, greatness and success in life to chance, I become intentional about my growth process.

777. I unleash the creative genius in me, I create and follow successful plans and strategies to accomplishing my prosperity.

778. I believe the answers to my prosperity and greatness lie within me, so launch down deep within me and begin to call the forth.

779. I speak words that build my self-confidence and self-esteem.

780. I intentional build successful relationships and dreams.

781. I speak words of truth, words of encouragement and words that affirms my worth.

782. I concentrate my attention on things that are of greatest priority in my journey to greatness and prosperity.

783. I focus my mental and verbal power on abundance and greatness, instead of lack and failure.

784. I am not afraid of rejection I will be successful and prosperous no matter the numbers and gravity of the rejections.

785. I refuse to imagine the worst, I feed my thoughts constantly on the best.

786. I focus more on what I have received and not being downcast because of things that are yet to be received.

787. My integrity are placed on high premium, I am a standard to emulate.

788. I live by my highest standard, situation

don't make me lose my principles towards success.
789. I maintain dignity and grace at all time and circumstances including times when pressure is at its peak.
790. I improve the quality of my experiences, negative experiences can't the zest for greatness in me.
791. I take responsibilities for all my actions and result.
792. As a successful person, I help others attain success by increasing their confidence and capacity.
793. I challenge my limiting belief about prosperity, success and greatness, and I positively come out of them.
794. All my investment are profitable, they attract prosperity to me.
795. God is my infinite supply, I can't be stranded on the path to prosperity and greatness.
796. I am making positive choices about what to do with my prosperity and greatness.
797. My wealth increase in every unforeseen ways.
798. I daily make a conscious commitment to be wealthy without bothering how possible it will be.
799. My experiences are the building blocks of my lifetime of remarkable successes and unending prosperity, I don't keep them as regrets.
800. I will keep launching out even if I don't see the whole path from the beginning, I will still keep moving.
801. I triumph in the face of fear.
802. I take a leap of faith towards success and my prosperity, I scale through every risks.
803. I keep knocking on every doors, until the

doors of greatness, success and prosperity open for me.
804. I will never give up on my hopes, dreams and ambitions, until I attain success.
805. I am empowered to lead a more fulfilling life.
806. I surround myself with successful people and not mediocre.
807. I consciously transform my dreams of success, greatness and prosperity into reality.
808. I take actions on what I desire in life, I don't leave them at the wish bank.
809. Success in all areas can be mine, I think and follow through the process until they are manifested.
810. I expand my opportunities tendencies, create new networks and get more out of every minute of my life.
811. I attract great people, great opportunities and fortunes into my life.
812. I step out of the demeaning culture of mediocrity and I create the life of my dreams.
813. I give up all my excuses and blame games, I receive the power to make a difference in life.
814. I say no to pressure of any kind.
815. I stop settling for less, I am big on the inside.
816. I stop living another man's dream, I discover the real me.
817. I aim high, I refuse to be talked out of my dreams, goals and vision.
818. I don't care what others think about me, I dare success and I will pursue it till I achieve it.
819. I use all experience to my successful advantage.
820. I am continuously and continually

improving on successful habits that lead to prosperity.

821. I see failure as temporary phase, they don't make me or define me.

822. I continually choose to have the right attitude towards the future.

823. I am a positive thinker, I cannot be associated with failure.

824. I am a creative being, I cause positive change in my life and environment.

825. I am persistent, I don't give in to challenges, I withstand challenges.

826. I am facing life with all confidence to succeed every day.

827. I am energetic in my pursuit of success, I shall prosper.

828. I forgo habits that negate prosperity.

829. I imbibe new and positive habits that promote prosperity.

830. I display my potentials for people to see, I attract the right kind of people, who will help me to be successful.

831. My success changes are without boarders because I commit to learning daily.

832. I am effortlessly surmounting all obstacles to my greatness.

833. My growth process is on the upward spiral, I am becoming a better version of myself daily.

834. I am not a doubter, I believe in myself and the process of greatness and prosperity I am going through.

835. I have an audacious zest for greatness, I look forward to new challenging successful endeavors.

836. I appreciate the greatness my life is turning into steadily.

837. My life is a bundle of opportunities for greatness, successes and prosperity.
838. My surrounding is an avenue for me to creatively make wealth and prosper.
839. I see clearly, in every of my challenges, I see the seeds of prosperity and greatness.
840. I am successful in everything I think or imagine.
841. I am well equipped for greatness and success.
842. I can always start again no matter how great and painful my losses are, failure cannot sink me.
843. I am surrounded by people with prosperity vibes.
844. I have foresight, I see opportunities in their raw states.
845. I am capable of being prosperous.
846. I am capable of impacting my world for good.
847. I am capable of being a motivation to myself and other people with my attitude to life and pursuit of success.
848. I celebrate success in others.
849. I have happy when others are prospering.
850. I always amplify excellence in other.
851. I always give my best, I display excellence in my words, attitudes and actions.
852. I am in irreplaceable, I have a lot in me to give to my world.
853. I am always optimistic, because every day is a new beginning of a success story for me.
854. I am hopeful of succeeding in every situation I find myself.
855. I am disciplined, I don't lose focus of my pursuit for greatness and success.

Master Key Series (Prosperity)

856. I do not stop to satisfy my pleasures, I push forward not forgetting my pursuit.
857. I do not put pleasure ahead of my pursuit of success and prosperity.
858. I am smart and I will keep taking the right actions towards success promptly.
859. I have no excuse in life because I have all it take to be great, successful and prosperous.
860. I would not allow procrastination deprive me of my prosperous future.
861. I would not allow laziness to hinder the manifestation of my visualize success.
862. I do not see impossibilities, I believe everything is possible including the actualization of my dreams.
863. I believe to be successful is not a mirage.
864. I believe greatness is attainable.
865. I do not label prosperity has impossible, in fact prosperity gravitates towards my life.
866. I consciously train my mind to see prosperity has my birth right.
867. I am my number one cheerleader to success, greatness and prosperity.
868. I release the wealth of prosperity deep within me and I direct them to achieving my greatness.
869. I have the ability to create my own world of prosperity.
870. I am impeccable in my thought life, my thoughts are flawless
871. I am an incredible thinker, my thoughts are extraordinary.
872. I am intentional in thought process, my thoughts process are greatness bound and I create successful realities.
873. All I think about is success and prosperity

and I am capable of achieving them in all facet of my life.

874. I am in total control of my thought pattern and action.

875. I do not fear failure.

876. I develop a burning desire for my pursuit in life and I will not stop directing my energy and resources towards my pursuit of all-round prosperity.

877. I get clarity of purpose, as I release my extraordinary for the good of mankind constantly.

878. I am a goal getter I cultivate the habit of daily setting realistic goals and strive to accomplish them.

879. I am my own rescue party, I do not create negative emotions towards prosperity.

880. I rise above the opinions of others and I become audacious in my quest for greatness, success and prosperity.

881. I am in charge of my emotions I keep a positive mind-set in every situation I find myself.

882. I am a builder of life I refuse to criticize, complain about and condemn people who have achieved and are achieving greatness in life.

883. I take the wheel of my life, I pilot myself to success and prosperity in every area of my life.

884. I pursue my true goals and I stop chasing shadows out of fear,

885. I feed my mind with the right information, I see the success and prosperity I desire.

886. I have an impeccable character that suits greatness, success and prosperity.

887. I set realistic goals I am firm in my pursuit but flexible to accept change.

888. I am open to new and evolving innovation and information that propels success and prosper-

ity.
889. I open to the realities of life, I appreciate the good ones but do not allow the bad ones to sink me, my purpose and pursuit.
890. I persist till I succeed no matter the harsh realities of life.
891. I evolve and grow to my full potentials, despites disappointments and setbacks.
892. I bounce back from every disappointments and setbacks.
893. I prosper in my spirit, I flourish beyond my imagination.
894. I prosper in my soul, my life attracts greatness.
895. I prosper in mind, I can't concede defeat.
896. I prosper in my finances, I cannot be poor.
897. I prosper in my body, I can't be cumbered with health challenges.
898. I prosper in my intellect, I am not dull mentally.
899. I prosper in my career, I see opportunities and utilize them rightly.
900. I prosper in my relationships, I add values to people connected to me directly and indirectly.
901. I prosper in my business, wealth magnet me even from unknown sources.
902. I focus on helping others succeed as I attain greatness.
903. I will keep trying different methods from lessons learnt from my failed efforts, I will not let them make me quit my quest for prosperity.
904. I cultivate a positive disposition towards life, I will not allow bad loss stop me from keep attempting success.
905. I look out for successful people, seek their success formulas and follow up with the formulas.

906. If others formulas do not work for me, I am determined to carve out new paths of success for myself.
907. I get help for every of my fears, I refuses to be without help, I embrace help and do things that will help me overcome my fears.
908. I surround myself with people who are capable of helping overcome my fears.
909. I will not base my success on speculations, I get the needed skills, knowledge and information for me to lead a successful life.
910. I do not ignore my fears, I face them and watch them shrink as I become prosperous.
911. I do not allow my fears paralyze me, they can inform my actions towards greatness but I do not allow them control my life.
912. I refuse to quit the path of prosperity in the face of challenges, I stay calm and think out mind blowing solutions.
913. I stay calm, I refuse to quit the path of greatness, I will not allow worries and anxiety control my decisions.
914. I stay calm, I refuse to quit the path of success, I will not let my stress level bend or break me.
915. I keep doing what is right to be done for me to be successful, even when it is not comfortable and I watch myself grow.
916. I keep my word and commitment to be great, successful and prosperous, even when it is not pleasurable.
917. I refuse to be depressed, when things don't come out the way I visualized them to be, I just keep trying again and again.
918. In my down moments, I will not lose myself because my mind is stronger than my emotions.

Master Key Series (Prosperity)

919. I do not allow my emotions to lead me, but my zeal propels me in this quest for prosperity.

920. I live above the noise, I will make sure I reach greatness, if I stumble and fall, I will pick myself up and continue my pursuit of prosperity.

921. I live above the noise of mockery and ridicule, they are not strong enough to stop my success quest.

922. My timing does not stop me, I might have started out late, I well persuaded that I am cut out for prosperity.

923. I begin to tackle every weaknesses in me that can destroy all the success I have striven to achieve in life.

924. I design the life I love to have and consciously work on my shortcomings.

925. I build a great team of success around me.

926. I prepare for my future with excitement, because I am assured of my prosperity no matter what it looks now.

927. I focus on the quality of the success I am becoming, not just the quantity of things I have achieved.

928. I raise my standards and I give myself value,

929. I am not ordinary, I am all shades of prosperity, success and greatness combined.

930. I am resourceful, I cannot be stuck on a spot.

931. I push myself daily to take calculated risk that help me solve problems.

932. I see every of my accomplishments as an avenue to do more.

933. I consciously make it a habit to always out do myself and my previous successes.

934. I train my mind to get ideas that will

launch me into prosperity.
935. I dare to be successful even if it will require me standing alone.
936. I don't beg for sympathy, I develop inner strength to follow after greatness.
937. I create the prosperous me I want to showcase to my world.
938. I am the one to create my success story, no one can do it better than I can.
939. I bear the pain growth and process of prosperity and success, I refuse to be stuck in penury.
940. I enjoy today's successes as I plough into tomorrow's greatness.
941. I forgo habits, actions, pleasures that are detrimental to my prosperity without guilt.
942. I do things can lead to my success, greatness and prosperity, I don't waste unnecessary time pondering over them.
943. I believe my best is yet to come, my present state is not my final bus stop.

944. I deserve happiness.
945. I deserve love.
946. I deserve light.
947. I deserve joy.
948. I deserve freedom.
949. I deserve to be loved.
950. I deserved to find a person who loves me for who I am.
951. I am worthy of attention.
952. I have a lot of chances for success.
953. My past and mistakes do not make who I will be.
954. I am a blessing to my world.
955. I am very skilled.

956. I am very wise.
957. I make progress every day.
958. I am developing a great and irresistible character daily.
959. I am handsome
960. I am great being me.
961. I love who I am.
962. I am becoming the kind of person I want to be.
963. I am having fun with my life.
964. The light is shining in me.
965. I am shinning every day.
966. Each day is blessed for me.
967. I am a happy person exuding happiness to the things and people around me.
968. I am developing my abilities daily.
969. I grow intentionally.
970. I am a global leader being molded every day.
971. I can learn fast.
972. I understand things quickly.
973. I am endowed with infinite intelligence.'
974. There is nothing I can't achieve once I set my mind to it.
975. I am evolving positively.
976. Negativity far from me.
977. I stay and speak positivity at all times.
978. I radiate positivism.
979. I crush it every day.
980. There is nobody who is like me.
981. I am unrivaled.'
982. I am a special breed with my own kind of intelligence.
983. I have an inexhaustibly intelligent mind.
984. My life is worth living.
985. My life makes loads of sense.

986. I am happy for the things I have achieved so far.
987. I am grateful for how far I have come.
988. I am grateful for the mistakes I made and the lessons I learnt.
989. I am happy for all the growth I have achieved so far.
990. I am grateful for my family.
991. I love the friends I have.
992. I am happy for the scars I have suffered and the victories that came afterwards.
993. I love who I am growing into becoming.
994. I have loving people around me.
995. My friends are kind to me.
996. My family loves me and I love them in return.
997. I have a life that is awesome.
998. I am a mad enthusiast.
999. Nothing can bring me down emotionally.
1000. I live a stupendously joyful life.
1001. I am bursting with life's energy.
1002. The ether works for me.
1003. I love peace and chase it with all men.
1004. I take over the reins of my emotions and I live happily with those who love me.
1005. I am valued and inspired to succeed.
1006. There is limitless energy inside me.
1007. I take charge of my emotions at all times.
1008. My body is beautiful and I love it.
1009. I have a razor-sharp mind that can understand things fast.
1010. I live for happiness always.
1011. I live for positivism every day.
1012. I attract the right people to me.
1013. I am courageously chasing my dreams.
1014. I am a confident in who I am.

1015. I feel confident all the time.
1016. I am continuously chasing my dreams and living my truth.
1017. My default mode is strength.
1018. I have for me and for those around me.
1019. I am a source of constant inspiration and hope.
1020. I laugh heartily at all times.
1021. I wear smile no matter the conditions around me.
1022. I am excited to be alive; I live this life to the fullest.
1023. My life is a gift and I am taking complete advantage of it.
1024. I live to my fullest potentials every day.
1025. My trajectory in life is upward and forward only.
1026. I will not falter.
1027. I will not fail.
1028. I am a miracle happening to my world.
1029. I know that my lines are falling unto me in pleasant places.
1030. I am a reason for people to love life.
1031. I will not fall.
1032. Confidence is my default setting.
1033. I look into the eyes of life and declare: you are working for my good.
1034. All that I require for life and success is inside me.
1035. I am self-driven and intrinsically motivated.
1036. I am a thermostat, I control the atmosphere around me.
1037. I am like black coffee, tough situations are designed to bring out the best in me.
1038. I will never fail.

1039. I stand on the shoulders of success.
1040. I have consistent success.
1041. I live in continuous success.
1042. I am a sun that illuminates the people and things around me.
1043. People remember for good.
1044. Feeling assured is a normal thing for me.
1045. I don't feel inferior no matter where I find myself.
1046. I am always creating ground-breaking art and work.
1047. My life is an art that people admire.
1048. I am admired and respected by the people around me and by those who know me.
1049. Every morning, I take giant leaps towards achieving my goals.
1050. There is a fountain of art, life and creativity that flows through me and out of me every single day of my life.
1051. I believe in the magic I am and the masterpiece I am becoming.
1052. No matter the number of times I fail, I will never accept the narrative of my bad situations.
1053. I am always striving for excellence and I achieve it and even more.

1054. I refuse to feel dejected.
1055. I refuse to feel alone.
1056. I refuse to feel worthless.
1057. I refuse to feel sad.
1058. I refuse to feel my life is a mess.
1059. I refuse the thoughts of suicide that plagues me.
1060. I do not accept I am a failure.
1061. I refute the thoughts that tell me I am

good for nothing.
1062. I refute the claims I am angry.
1063. I am striving for peace.
1064. I am a peaceful person.
1065. I do not accept what this feeling says.
1066. I am worthy of beauty in my life.
1067. I am not a mistake neither are my thoughts.
1068. The things I create are valid.
1069. The art I create is worthy of emulation.
1070. I am not afraid of the art I create.
1071. People gravitate towards my art.
1072. I am an amazingly creative being.
1073. I do not live in hate.
1074. I do not live in anger.
1075. I do not live with resentment.
1076. I do not live with bitterness.
1077. I do not live with regrets.
1078. I live a life of sweetness.
1079. I live a life of appreciation.
1080. I love a life of unending happiness.
1081. I live a joy-filled life.
1082. My whole being is saturated with love.
1083. I love with no restraints.
1084. I am not a wicked person.
1085. I do not hold on to hurts.
1086. I let go of all pains.
1087. I do not make enemies.
1088. I make friends.
1089. I am friendly and likeable.
1090. I do not hold on to past hurts from people I love.
1091. I forgive easily.
1092. I forgive completely.
1093. I forgive quickly.
1094. I forgive with all my heart.

1095. Past wrongs don't hold me back.
1096. I let go of hurts and move on with love.
1097. I love my enemies.
1098. I pray for them like my friends.
1099. I love the people who have hurt me.
1100. I love the people who broke my heart.
1101. I love the lessons I learnt from those mistakes.
1102. I appreciate the people whose lives taught me patience.
1103. I appreciate the people whose hurts taught me love.
1104. I appreciate the people who understand me.
1105. I appreciate the people whose heart has held mine in their palms.
1106. I am a love being who constantly loves with reckless abandon.
1107. I appreciate the people who loved me at my worse.
1108. I appreciate the ears that listened to me on my bad days.
1109. I am grateful for the people who loved me in my flawed state.
1110. I am not a broken person.
1111. I find healing in life.
1112. I find peace in the world around me.
1113. I am growing in peace.
1114. I do not live in fear of the unknown.
1115. I have heaven inside me.
1116. Laughter lines my face at all times.
1117. I have a boundless stream of happiness flowing through me.
1118. I take charge of my heart and stay focused.
1119. I am growing into a love being.
1120. The energy of life, boundless energy, flows

in me and through me.
1121. It takes me nothing to let go of hurt.
1122. I stay calm in tough situations.
1123. I face challenging situations with calmness.
1124. The storms do not throw me off balance.
1125. The storms propel me to greater things.
1126. The storms propel me to higher heights.
1127. The storms are meant to help me progress.
1128. The storms are winds I have yet learnt how to control.
1129. Greater is my ability to control pain than the pain to control me.
1130. I rise above bigotry.
1131. I rise above pain.
1132. I rise above sorrow.
1133. I rise above disdain for life.
1134. I rise above poverty of the mind.
1135. I rise above hurts.
1136. I am rising above negative energies,
1137. I welcome light.
1138. I welcome peace,
1139. I welcome love.
1140. I welcome colors in my life.
1141. I welcome wholesome forgiveness.
1142. I welcome moving forward.
1143. I welcome emotional growth.
1144. I welcome progress.
1145. I welcome emotional stability.
1146. I embrace hope in my life.
1147. I embrace living.
1148. I live my life to its fullest.
1149. Joy has no bounds in my life.
1150. Peace lives with me.
1151. I am destined for great things.
1152. I walk in the love of god.

1153. My soul is filled with colors of life.
1154. I enjoy this gift of life.
1155. I live my truth to the fullest.
1156. I am not apologetic for who I am.
1157. My whole being radiates colors of happiness.
1158. I don't find it hard to love my enemies.
1159. My efforts are yielding results.
1160. I am rewarded for my hard work.
1161. People recognize my diligence.

1162. I am prosperous, no matter the situation and things am struggling with.
1163. I walk away from people and situations that threatens my self-worth and self-value.
1164. I do not see my ideas to people that will make light of my dreams, I only communicate them to like minds.
1165. I make myself a priority, not people's opinions or reactions.
1166. I am fearless in my pursuit of success.
1167. I refuse to stay on a spot, I have faith in God to help solve the mystery of life, as I pursue prosperity.
1168. I step out daily in faith, trusting to scale through the day successfully, no matter, how hard the day before was.
1169. I stop comparing myself with others, I define what success is, by doing it my own way.
1170. I do not harbor resentment, I do not hold on to guilt and anger of past mistakes and experiences, because they do not suit my prosperous status.
1171. I celebrate the abundance within me i see prosperity boosting out of me to my worry.

1172. I am conscious of my value, i can't be anything less than greatness.
1173. I deserve every success and prosperity that happens in my life, my life is not a product of chance.
1174. I faith in my plans to be prosperous, i will follow them though with all zeal.
1175. I am worthy of my accomplishments, more outstanding heights am yet to attain.
1176. In me is residence all it takes for me be great, be prosperous and also extend it to others around me.
1177. I have limitless abilities to become successful despite my condition.
1178. I have so many options to choose from, am not stranded of ideas to creating wealth.
1179. I am empowered to confront any problem, that threatens my prosperity.
1180. I make the best use of my time, i don't sell myself cheap.
1181. I choose to succeed against all odds
1182. I choose to be great beyond my imaginations
1183. I choose to prosper despite the distraction on my path
1184. I free from the chains of fear, i am victorious.
1185. I am an inspiration to many of the journey to greatness.
1186. I am consistence in my strive for prosperity.
1187. I persevere amidst turbulent challenges of life to attain greatness.
1188. At every phase of my life i learn lessons that aids my success, greatness and prosperity.
1189. I keep building on my momentums

through focus.
1190. I have all it take to excel in life
1191. I have all i require to success in life
1192. I am up to the task to meet the demands of greatness
1193. I am capable of paying the price for me to be prosperous in this life.
1194. I do not waste my energy on success deflators.
1195. I overcome every distraction to my prosperity
1196. I overcome every distractions to my greatness
1197. I overcome every distraction to my succeeding
1198. I receive strength to deal with the issues of life.
1199. I stall calm in the midst of storms
1200. I keep moving, i stride the path of prosperity with all the confidence i have got.

1201. I can go beyond my fears and limitations

1202. I take charge of my life

1203. My happiness is my choice

1204. I am living my best life

1205. I am bold and courageous

1206. I take each day at a time, and I make it count

1207. My self-development is key

1208. I am in no competition with anybody other than who I was yesterday

1209. I am undeterred, even if I'm faced with a defeat, I shall rise again, like a phoenix

1210. I am not intimidated by anyone, for I'm the best version of myself

1211. No matter what life throws at me, I'm a conqueror

1212. Life is fair to me

1213. I rule my world

1214. I enjoy life and all the goodness it has for me

1215. Life favours me and all that I do

1216. I take root, and I am deeply grounded

1217. I might bend, but I would not break

1218. I would not dim my light, I'll keep shining my light to the world

1219. I am a beautiful expression of life

1220. I am here to be Me

1221. I am here to shine my unique light

1222. I am lovingly speaking my truth

1223. I forgive those who have hurt in the past. I let them go. I am setting myself free.

1224. I now have peace with myself.

1225. I henceforth live in love and exude love

1226. I enjoy sanity of my mind, spirit and body

1227. I am not consumed by anger

1228. I heal myself of past hurts and pain

1229. As I forgive myself, it becomes easier to forgive others

1230. I am willing to let go, deep within me is an infinite well of love

1231. I forgive those who have hurt and peacefully let them go in my mind

1232. I forgive myself and set myself free, I say yes to life and life says yes to me

1233. I forgive myself for not being perfect

1234. The past is gone, and it has no power over me, I live in the present

1235. Starting now I am free, I create my thoughts

1236. I forgive myself of any mistakes that I made

1237. I am grateful for my life

1238. I am thankful for the gift of today

1239. I am grateful for the gift of family and of friends

1240. I am grateful for the air I breathe

1241. I am grateful for the gift of nature

1242. I am thankful for my partner

1243. I am grateful for my children

1244. My life is filled with appreciation and gratitude

1245. I am grateful for the small things and big things

1246. My day begins with gratitude and ends with it

1247. I am thankful for my job

1248. I am grateful for my environment

1249. I grateful for the well of love that springs up within me

1250. I am thankful for my business and my customers

1251. I am grateful for the strength to keep pushing on

1252. I am thankful for the lessons I have learnt in life

1253. I am grateful for all my mistakes

1254. I am grateful for where I am today

1255. I am thankful for where I am headed

1256. I am grateful for the processes involved in my growth

1257. I am grateful for the opportunities I lost and the ones that I have

1258. I am aware of who I am becoming, and I am thankful

1259. I am genuinely grateful for the chance to choose

1260. I am awakening to the potential within me, and I am thankful

1261. I am thankful for this remarkable journey in my body

1262. I am so happy and grateful for all the freedom to be myself

1263. I am valuable, thank you

1264.

1265. I am at peace with myself

1266. I peacefully detach myself from negative people

1267. I am in harmony with my environment

1268. I find peace with my job

1269. I enjoy peace always

1270. Everything around me brings me peace

1271. I am made to do great things

1272. I am blessed with infinity talents, and I use them every day

1273. I can achieve great things in my life

1274. I am productive

1275. I am filled with energy and determination

1276. I am in control of everything that I think or do

1277. I am made for more

1278. I can do anything I put my heart to do

1279. I am unstoppable

1280. I am a conqueror

1281. My dreams are valid and achievable

1282. I am limitless

1283. I am champion

1284. I am the world's greatest

1285. I am an overcomer

1286. I am courageous

1287. I am in charge

1288. I am celebrated

1289. I am magnificent

1290. I am dedicated

1291. I am decisive

1292. Each day I completely trust my intuition

1293. Each day is a gift, and I gratefully accept it

1294. I give my best to each day, and I live it at best

1295. I take each as it comes

1296. I am not overwhelmed by any situation of today

1297. Today I allow myself to shine and I honor the best part of me, and I share them with others

1298. My energy and vitality increases each and every day

1299. My well-being is my priority today and always

1300. I choose today to follow my heart, and I discover my destiny

1301. I choose simplicity and peace today

1302. Today I allow myself to be stronger than my fears

1303. Today I create harmony, peace, and joy for myself

1304. I choose to be authentic today

1305. I am enlightened

1306. Today I am vibrant

1307. I am smart

1308. I am humorous

1309. I am fully present

1310. I am aware

1311. Today I take responsibility for my actions

1312. I am engaging, enjoyable

1313. I am self-assured

1314. I am helpful

1315. I am an eager student

1316. Today I am competent

1317. I am fair

1318. I am discerning

1319. I am focused

1320. I attract an abundance of wealth into my life

1321. I can make as much money as I choose to

1322. I am worthy of abundance in all my endeavors

1323. My thoughts are filled with an abundance of wealth

1324. I can handle abundant success

1325. I attract abundance and happiness

1326. Prosperity surrounds me, Prosperity fulfills me, and Prosperity flows towards me and through me

1327. My life is filled with prosperity

1328. I am richly blessed, wealth continually comes into my life

1329. I am a magnet attracting abundance in my life

1330. I am successful in every area of my life

1331. I am not held down by the thoughts of poverty

1332. I receive all the wealth the world has to offer

1333. I am deeply grateful for the wealth in my life

1334. I am not in confinement, my wealth is limitless

1335. All my relationships have a purpose, and they fulfill me

1336. I am always happy for other people

1337. I attract long-lasting friendships into my life

1338. I allow others simply to be themselves, I cannot change another person

1339. I accept everyone around me

1340. I am polite and respectful to any person that I meet

1341. I am blessed with an incredible family and beautiful friends

1342. I happily build a healthy relationship

1343. Others are attracted to me because of my positive energy

1344. I deserve a loving and long-lasting relationship

1345. I find peace in my relationship

1346. I am divinely guided into the most loving relationship that life has to offer

1347. Everything that I do serves my goals without affecting others

1348. I am focused on the present

1349. I focus on the good in any given situation

1350. I am fully committed to achieving my goals.

1351. I believe in my abilities.

1352. I am reliable, determined and focused.

1353. I am consistent.

1354. I take action towards achieving my goals.

1355. I am free from self-doubt.

1356. I honor my commitments

1357. Nothing will stop me from accomplishing my goal.

1358. I am endowed with all the power to reach all my goals

1359. I am well and able to achieve all my goals

1360. I am undeterred

1361. It always seems impossible, but it is possible

1362. I am dedicated to finishing all my projects.

1363. I am energized to get all my projects done.

1364. I am full of energy.

1365. I am motivated and driven.

1366. I can finish all my tasks.

1367. I am a highly productive person.

1368. I have intense concentration.

1369. I am focused and determined to get more done.

1370. I can tackle any task in front of me.

1371. My mind is clear and focused.

1372. I am present in this moment.

1373. Nothing distracts me.

1374. My focus is getting better every day.

1375. I am becoming a focused person.

1376. I am free from distractions.

1377. Being focused comes easily to me.

1378. I am focused on the task at hand.

1379. One day at a time. One step at a time.

1380. I get things done fast.

1381. I never put things off.

1382. I am a doer.

1383. I act quickly.

1384. I am motivated to finish my tasks.

1385. I have the willpower to do my assignments.

1386. I am a proactive person.

1387. I finish my projects effortlessly.

1388. I love taking action.

1389. Nothing will stand in my way of accomplishing my tasks.

1390. No excuses. Just results.

1391. Every day I am moving my life forward.

1392. I am determined to get everything done.

1393. I enjoy completing my tasks.

1394. I keep growing stronger

1395. I am truthful

1396. I am trustworthy

1397. I am well equipped for the task of the day

1398. I have confidence in my abilities

1399. I make every second of each day count

1400. I am patient

1401. I am far superior to negative thoughts and low actions

1402. I am competent in my work

1403. I am organized and disciplined

1404. I am not laid back

1405. As I go to work today, I am powered to do great things.
1406. No task is too difficult for me to complete at work today.
1407. I feel great about the work I am going to do because I am adding value to humanity.
1408. I have within me the great wisdom of the world inside of me. I am going to dispense some of that wisdom at work today.
1409. I am doing an excellent job because I am able to and I have the strength to.
1410. I am going to make tremendous impact today at work.
1411. The work I do is meaningful and I am part of that meaning.
1412. There is nothing too hard for me to do

today; therefore, I do all my work excellently.

1413. I know sometimes tough tasks await me, but these tough tasks are to test my brilliance, of which I have an abundance of.

1414. Taking the next step in my life means taking myself to work because the work I do matter in the long run.

1415. If I can choose this day which work I want to do, I will choose this one, always.

1416. There is beauty in adding beauty to the world, and my job gives me the chance to.

1417. I am an artiste, painting the world with beautiful colors of my work.

1418. I feel fulfilled and contented with the work I do,

1419. I love my coworkers. I love my boss. My work environment inspires me to do the best and be the best version of myself.

1420. I take nothing for granted, my job is one of those things; it matters I did my best at all times.

1421. There are no better jobs in the world aside this one I have.

1422. Although this is not the place I want to be, this phase of my life, this job, is a vehicle that is taking me there and I am going to enjoy this journey.

1423. This job makes me super happy because I am doing what I like with people I love.

1424. I can't wait to get to work and crush it. I have enormous energy inside me, I need to dispense it at work today.

1425. What I am going to do at work is so great I can't wait to get started.

1426. This job makes so much sense to me I am pumped to get on with it.

1427. This work is so exciting that I can do this

all day, for the rest of my life

1428. I am on top of the world just thinking of my job.

1429. I create beauty at work all day.

1430. This is best job in the world.

1431. There was never a better time to be alive and be doing this job.

1432. I was made for this job, and I am doing it perfectly.

1433. I know today isn't going as planned, but I am sure it would end well because I say so.

1434. Whatever is thrown at me today at work, I devour for dinner.

1435. I am excellent at what I do.

1436. I have no fear what magnitude of work is thrown at me today, I am more than able to do them well.

1437. Working with these guys has to be the best thing in the world.

1438. Sometimes I wonder why I get paid for doing such an insanely sweet job.

1439. I work because I know my work adds tremendous value to the world around me.

1440. I am motivated to work today; I have infinite intelligence to do it.

1441. Work is not hard; I just need to push myself farther than I am used to.

1442. This work is doable! And I am doing it with brilliance.

1443. There is so much inside me the world needs to have a taste of; let's get to work.

1444. I believe I have it within me to finish this task I have started, and I will finish.

1445. If anybody can do this work well, it is me, and I am doing it perfectly.

1446. This work is not difficult for me! This work

is not difficult for me! This work is not difficult for me!

1447. I have boundless energy to boundless work and these works count.

1448. I have infinite intelligence! It is coming to the fore today at work.

1449. Whenever I think of the work I do, I feel I've been mightily blessed.

1450. Nothing can stop me from doing my best at all times.

1451. I give the best there is of me whenever I am called to do a job.

1452. I do such a great job, I am super proud of myself.

1453. If anything goes wrong, I am more than capable of fixing it.

1454. Calm down! Calm down! This is a hurdle you were created to surpass.

1455. It doesn't make sense now, but I'll keep trying, I am sure it'll make sense as I move forward.

1456. I am a global leader in my field.

1457. I never settle for less than what is excellent!

1458. I am doing this now because there is something greater ahead of me; I need this to excel at the one in the future.

1459. I love my job!

1460. I am always creating magnificent content my clients can't help but be wowed.

1461. This has always been my dream,. And I am living it to the fullest.

1462. What adds color to the world cannot cause me to feel depressed; I am above these awful feelings.

1463. Today, I place my best food forward and

that foot is taking giant strides.
1464. I am more than enough for this job I am going for.

1465. I was made for this job!
1466. Whatever questions I will be asked, I am acing it without breaking a sweat.
1467. There is something about me that my would-be employees can't help but like.
1468. I am what this position has been looking for all its life.
1469. For all the things I am good at, this job is one of my strongest.
1470. I am not afraid of who would be interviewing me because I am prepared to answer their questions correctly.
1471. I have the skills to nail down this job; let's go get it!
1472. I am amazed at how well I can do this job.
1473. There has never been a better candidate for a job than me for this job.
1474. I walk in there with confidence because I know my onions.
1475. I find favor in the eyes of my interviewers.
1476. This job is available to me and I will get it.
1477. The light I carry inside me illuminates so brightly my employees also get illuminated.
1478. This work is mine and mine to take.
1479. I have the skills needed to do a brilliantly awesome job.
1480. There is a nothing impossible for me to do at this job.
1481. I am going to get this job! I have the intelligence needed to get this job!
1482. When I enter the office, my light would

draw my employees in.

1483. My new co-workers love me even if they haven't met me.

1484. There has never been a better time to start work with these people.

1485. I believe in my abilities to impact my co-workers positively.

1486. I am anxious.

1487. I am highly skilled and emotionally stable.

1488. There is no task I can't surmount.

1489. It would take time, effort and dedication; but I'll get it done.

1490. My mind is alert to goodness and I give it all the time.

1491. The mind I have is blessed with light, I do not allow hate and darkness fill it.

1492. I work with the best people there are; smart and god fearing.

1493. My boss is a wonderful person, he understand me perfectly.

1494. I give my best and my best is appreciated.

1495. There surely would be need for hardening for diamond to be formed, this process is my hardening and I am coming out a glittering diamond.

1496. I am created for excellence, all the time.

1497. From the work I do, I send out light and love to the world around me, including the people with whom I interact.

1498. If I ever fail, I am failing forward.

1499. I take the bull by the horn because the bull is mine and I have control over it.

1500. Why should I be afraid when I am intelligent and perfect for the job?

1501. I'll take this job that I have been offered, my energy is what they have been looking for.

1502. Even in the midst of the storm, I soar.
1503. No matter what happens today as I step out for this interview, I am still a winner.
1504. Every disappointment is another step that takes me closer to my destiny.
1505. I am not afraid of whatever may happen, I am more than a conqueror.
1506. I have the great wisdom of God inside me, therefore I fear nothing.
1507. I am an eagle soaring above the hate around me.
1508. I am stronger than the disappointments.
1509. I make ends meet, and far from that even, I have the ability to make wealth.
1510. From the depth of my soul, I release the light of the world to the people around me.
1511. I insist on my rights

1512. If anything goes wrong, it is going wrong because something better awaits me in the future; and I am ready to take the future.
1513. Why should I bother when something doesn't work? Because all things work together for my good.
1514. For all the elements of the world are aligning for my good, therefore I bask in my success.
1515. Success is not an event, it is a process. I therefore trust this process, no matter how herculean it may seem.
1516. I know that good things come just after the darkest night; I'll wait for the morning.
1517. Every day is an opportunity to become like god, good or bad, I am unfolding into god.
1518. Take away all the light in the world; I'll still shine because I am an endless light that can't

be snuffed out.

1519. There is a world inside me that world outside me can't get enough of; let's unleash our beauty to the world!

1520. Make no mistake, I'll make mistakes, but I am not my mistakes. My mistakes are lyrics for my victory song.

1521. Truth be told, I am bold!

1522. My new employees can't wait to have me work for them.

1523. I am loved and liked by all I come across today.

1524. Nothing has the power to make me feel inferior, I am superior always.

1525. I have the wisdom to do all that is required of me, nothing is impossible for me to do.

1526. I am not depressed, I am happy.

1527. I know this feeling is just for a while, this too will pass.

1528. I am not my emotions, I live above how I feel.

1529. I am a happy person, bursting with life all the time.

1530. I have such stable mind it can withstand any storm.

1531. This storm has nothing on me, I'll ride it to victory.

1532. I am not useless, I just feel like I am.

1533. How I feel is not who I am.

1534. I feel great even if my emotions say otherwise.

1535. I matter to the world and in the world.

1536. There is nothing that can put me down, I have infinity inside me.

1537. Today, I tap from existential life that resides in me, and I do exploits.
1538. There is goodness inside me and it shows forth.
1539. I am a light and I shine tirelessly.
1540. I am a lyric so sweet the world can't do without me.
1541. I am not depressed, I don't care how I feel, I am not depressed.
1542. I have people who love me for who I am and what I represent.
1543. There is light in this tunnel for me.
1544. I will never allow this speck of darkness overpower the light inside of me.
1545. Sadness is not a home I choose to stay in, I leave now!
1546. There is a fountain of joy welled up inside me; the water flows now!
1547. Take a look at me; I have the life of god inside me.
1548. I take charge of my emotions and I declare I am excited.
1549. My life is important and I know it.
1550. I am living my best life each day.
1551. Even though it doesn't feel like it, I am breaking forth and singing.
1552. I have a volcano of happiness erupting right now,
1553. I am so super happy I can't help myself.
1554. There is this joy so strong, brewing like volcano.
1555. I have the life of god inside me; I have no reason to be fear.
1556. I have hope. I have love. I have life.
1557. I have faith in who I am and what I am becoming.

1558. I know that this is a process, and I am unfolding into a flower so beautiful.
1559. I take my stand today and declare I am filled with energy.
1560. There is nothing stopping me today, I break forth and shine.
1561. I am the sun; I shine in all I do.
1562. I expel every form of darkness lurking; I am light shining brightly!
1563. I have the joy that flows like a river inside me.
1564. I declare I am joyful.
1565. I make bold to say today that the lines of life is falling unto me into pleasant place.
1566. I have light inside me, not darkness, not sadness.
1567. I love who I am and I am enjoying who I am becoming.
1568. I know this is just a phase of my life, and I am coming out of it stronger than I entered.
1569. Good habits are hard to form but easy to live with, therefore I form the habit of always staying happy irrespective of the things happening around me.
1570. The things around me will not affect the things inside me; I choose to stay positive even in the midst of external turmoil.
1571. I am not depressed. I reject that label.
1572. I have no pain inside me, none at all.
1573. I am a forgiving person; I forgive all those who have hurt me.
1574. I have the joy of the lord inside me.
1575. I am special to my family; they love me with a boundless energy that can't be quantified.
1576. I take over the reins of my emotions today and declare I am on top of the world with joy.

1577. I have joy overflow like a river.
1578. The joy of the lord is my strength.
1579. I take hold of all the light in the world, channeling them into me for good.
1580. All things work together for my good.
1581. I am the light of the world, I shine!
1582. My life is beautiful, always has and always will be because I am the light of this world.
1583. I soar above the pain I feel.
1584. I am a lion, I win all the time.
1585. I am bold and over joyous.

1586. I failed today doesn't make a failure, it's just a stumbling block.
1587. I am coming back stronger and better from this failed trial.
1588. The best people in the world have failed; I am on my way to greatness.
1589. Greatness isn't achieved on a whim, it takes time and lessons.
1590. I have not failed until I tell myself I am a failure, and I am not a failure.
1591. I didn't fail, I just learnt a new way to try again, better informed.
1592. If I don't fail, how do I have stories to tell when I succeed?
1593. I know people think this failure is all there is to me, but only if they could see the light just behind the horizon, they'll know why I am so happy.
1594. I believe this chance I failed is a door to better things for me.
1595. I dare to say I'll rather fail and learn than not fail at all and stay at a place; so let's go, we fail forward!

Master Key Series (Prosperity)

1596. How would I know the depth of my strength if I don't try? I tried this, I failed, let us give it a better shot this time.

1597. I have learnt a new way not to try doing this task; it would make a good book.

1598. I have the title for my first book: how I failed and didn't stop at it.

1599. If you looked at the wind, you won't sew. If I look at the failings, I won't move. We move!

1600. I take a bottle of hope for every time life has tried to kill me but failed.

1601. This battle has been lost, I will win the war in the end, let's keep going baby.

1602. Because the road is tough doesn't mean the journey won't be completed; I do this and I do it right irrespective.

1603. I pass through fire because I am gold that needs refining.

1604. Even though I walk through the valley of death, fear no failure because victory is sure.

1605. Nothing can snuff out the light inside me, not even this temporary failure.

1606. Failure is temporary; my acceptance is what's permanent. I choose not to allow that.

1607. Nothing stick except I permit it, therefore I do not permit this failure as final.

1608. This failure isn't fatal; I still have my breath to go at it.

1609. What doesn't kill me can only scar me; I wear those scars as my trophy for when I win.

1610. I take charge of my life and declare that this failure is not final.

1611. I have a burning desire that can't be quenched by this small setback.

1612. I realize I just failed at something that I love, and I know it feels like this is the end, but I won't stop.

1613. This is not the end. This can never be the end. I see a brighter future just waiting for me to take a hold of.

1614. There is nothing impossible for me to do, and I am not accepting this task is one of the impossible things for me. I will win the end, I win!

1615. Hear me failure: you met the wrong guy; I keep moving and breaking down walls.

1616. I am never going back to what I have started, I keep moving forward irrespective.

1617. There is nothing I cannot surmount, not even this setback.

1618. I know what I want, and I am empowered to achieve it no matter what happens.

1619. Hurdles are not meant to stop me, they are meant to be surpassed. I will jump past this hurdle.

1620. I failed doesn't mean I will not succeed. This is only but a phase I am prepared to walk through.

1621. Even though I walk through the valley of shadow of death, I fear no evil.

1622. I am confident this setback is only but for a while.

1623. There is a place for failing; I know that therefore I am not taking this failure too personal.

1624. I wish things were different and I had succeeded, but I am not going to let this stop me from moving forward.

1625. I take the bold step today, declaring victory in the midst of this recent failure.

1626. I am highly motivated to try again, and again, and again, until I am successful.

1627. I am never stopping till I get this thing done; failure doesn't have enough power to stop me.

1628. If I quit now, what would I tell all the gifts dormant inside me? That I stopped because of a small test? There are bigger fishes to fry, so we keep moving forward!

1629. Quitters never win, winners have no business quitting. I am a winner, I have no business quitting.

1630. I am not stopping till I win.

1631. The universe is working to make all things work for my good.

1632. If this is all life has got for me, then we are going to have a jolly good ride 'cause I am not giving up anytime soon, not now, not ever!

1633. Hey life, throw your best shot, I am more than prepared for you.

1634. Even if I fail a thousand times, I still over a thousand more trials to make it right; make it right I will.

1635. This blow is not unto death, therefore I will keep fighting till I achieve what I want.

1636. Dear life, I am bloodied, I have not tapped out, I am never going to. So you either answer me now or answer me later, any which ways, you will give me what I want.

1637. I am not leaving this world unfulfilled. I must and I will achieve all my set goals.

1638. I declare I am more than a conqueror all the days of my life.

1639. Sing my soul! Rejoice 'because you have failed again I am now closer to your destiny.

1640. I am fulfilling destiny in this life.

1641. The lines of the world are falling unto me in pleasant and beautiful laces.

1642. The stars and the elements of the world are aligning for me, so I am not bothered about this time I failed.

1643. If I stop, there would be no crown to be worn at the end. I keep running.

1644. I complete the task set before me, striving for the higher calling and attaining the highest heights possible.

1645. I am enough! More than able to outlive this failure and do much more.

1646. Now, I take hold of success and decree it unto my work!

1647. I am not overweight; I eat right and eat healthy.

1648. I am living a healthy life in my diet.

1649. I can and I will exercise because I love myself.

1650. I love my body and I will treat it right.

1651. I eat healthy today and always.

1652. My life and my future needs my body to be fit, and I will make it so.

1653. For myself, for my family and those who love me, I will stay and eat well.

1654. I realize how difficult it is to keep off snacks, but this life of mine is filled with too much blessing to allow overweight steal it from me.

1655. I am happy with who I am.

1656. I don't hate my body! I don't hate my body! I don't hate my body!

1657. I have a great body even behind this seemingly overweight one I am currently carrying.

1658. Irrespective of what they say about me, I am a great person; I am not defined by my body size.

1659. I am proud of who I am and I am happy with my damn body!

1660. Today is the start of something new happening to me.
1661. I am a happy fat person.
1662. My friends and family and colleagues love me for who I am and what I represent.
1663. I know how uncomfortable my body weight is, and I am doing all I can to live right.
1664. I am body positive and I am getting better.
1665. I ate too much today, it's just a setback and it doesn't define me and my journey to living healthy.
1666. It has never been easy, but I have come this far, I'll keep going.
1667. I am ready to sweat out this excess fat.
1668. I am doing this for me and not for any other human.
1669. Losing weight is all about me and how I feel about myself; not about another person or the society.
1670. Eating at the right time and the correct nutrient is something I am happy doing.
1671. My body is not a disease; nobody has the right to make me feel that way.
1672. I am excited about how fit I am becoming.
1673. The sweating at the gym is a price I am a ready to pay.
1674. I take up a healthy lifestyle and I see it through no matter the hurdles before me.
1675. I am a happy person burning with endless desire to lose my excess weight.
1676. I have a weight goal that I am achieving irrespective of what people say.
1677. There is no failure that is too fatal to recover from, therefore I am taking this weight bull by the horn and I am riding to fitness.
1678. I am lose weight today!

1679. I am strong enough to go through the rigors of my physical exercise.
1680. My mind is alert and fit for the journey of weight loss.
1681. Since I am alive, I therefore can burn these calories.
1682. I declare that I am disciplined enough to avoid the food I should and do the thing I should do.
1683. Losing weight is not impossible for me, i can do it!
1684. Just like Nike said, just do it! Just do it!
1685. I am strong, fair and upright.
1686. Justice is being done to my body as I put it under the rigors of physical exercise.
1687. Dear body, I own you! Therefore I can and will push you back to fitness as I deem fit.
1688. Take this from me: I am not returning to my old eating habits.
1689. I have the power within me to live healthy; I am living healthy.
1690. I obey the food timetable that has been set for me. I follow throw religiously and I see significant improvement in my weight.
1691. I take pride in the beauty of my mind and my body; I am lo0oking great.
1692. I failed today doesn't make me a failure in this journey to weight loss. I try again.
1693. I keep moving forward toward becoming the kind of person I have also wanted to be and having the kind of body that allows me live my best life.
1694. Never again am I going back to hating myself and my beautiful body.
1695. I am a light! My body is a temple! Only learned priest can ever understand the sacrament

that it is!

1696. Nothing can break this body of mine into an apology. I am loud music.

1697. I am the sweetest song on the lips of angels; my body is the hymn book; can you see the lines of god written on my flesh?

1698. Look at me as purposefully as you want, this flesh is what god looks like. '

1699. People only criticize what they know nothing about. I am the secret god has been keeping to his chest; see my heavenly body.

1700. I know being fat is unhealthy, but I also know not loving myself kills me faster than these calories can. So today, I take over the reins of my happiness and declare my body fit for living and existing.

1701. I enjoy each single day in this big house called my body.

1702. I am fit. I am strong. I live healthy!

1703. My body is the temple of god, no more would I defy it with overfeeding.

1704. I will go to the gym today and I will burn out significant number of pounds.

1705. I agree that it hard, exercising and eating right, but I also know I have it within me to surpass the toughness. I am more than able to.

1706. I boldly declare: this body of mine is a holy prayer!

1707. I am good enough for the right person.

1708. I have the fountain of love flowing endlessly within me, I am not allowing anybody make me feel less.

1709. When I am here, I am here in the present, not in the past, not in the future. I am here now and that is enough.

1710. I am enough light for the world to have; he left because he can't see well.

1711. I am enough! I am more than enough! I am too enough!

1712. She left because she wanted not because I was a bad person.

1713. This love was a journey; it's time to move on to better things and people.

1714. It was great while it lasted, but my life is meant to move forward and upward only.

1715. I take charge of how I feel; nobody will make me hate myself.

1716. I am full of hope and love and peace and happiness and laughter and all that is beautiful in the world.

1717. My heart is not broken, it only misses you. But not to worry, it has learnt to love itself all by itself.

1718. My world is good enough for my heart.

1719. Dear heart, you are strong, don't ever forget that.

1720. I don't regret falling in love and loving with all of my being; that's what life is about.

1721. Giving me out to love, wholly, was splendid while it lasted. Now that it has ended, let us move on to higher grounds.

1722. She was never meant to be, it is no fault of yours.

1723. I will laugh like a child, nothing and no one can still my childlike innocence from me, not even heartbreak.

1724. I am at ease with all the uncontrollable things happening in my life

1725. I make good decisions
1726. I am a positive person
1727. I am reliable
1728. I am healthy
1729. I am important
1730. I am respected
1731. I am competent in my daily tasks
1732. I am loved
1733. I am a miracle
1734. I am greatly endowed with life
1735. I am a force of creation
1736. I am a unique blend of love and power
1737. I am a force to reckon with
1738. I am charming
1739. I am gracious
1740. I am marvelous
1741. I am radiant
1742. I am a creative and innovative human being
1743. I am a loving human being
1744. I am intelligent
1745. I am a fighter, I refuse to give up!
1746. I am valuable
1747. I am the only one who can stop me
1748. Everything is good right here right now
1749. I am loyal

1750. I respect myself, and everything that I do is meant to fulfill me

1751. I am open-minded

1752. I take full advantage of all opportunity surrounding me

1753. I choose to see all the opportunity surrounding me

1754. Everything that I need comes to me at the right moment

1755. I focus on the good in any given situation

1756. I am aware of my mistakes, and I learn from them

1757. I make good decisions

1758. I feel admiration for everything surrounding me

1759. I am inspired with new and useful ideas

1760. I am content but not complacent with all my accomplishments

1761. I am kind

1762. I am a positive person

1763. I am reliable

1764. I am a compassionate being

1765. I am a learner

1766. I am a curious being

1767. My inner voice is always positive in any given situation

1768. I completely trust myself, I can easily say no when I need to

1769. I am in complete control of every aspect of my life

1770. I find it easy to continually work hard

1771. I create my own success

1772. I react with wisdom to every challenge that comes my way

1773. I believe in the power of positive thinking

1774. I am important

1775. I am respected

1776. I am competent in my daily tasks

1777. My mind is powerful it can make wishes come through

1778. I am humbled and always ready to learn

1779. I react with love in any given situation

1780. I am loved

1781. I am a miracle

1782. Happiness is present in each of my thoughts

1783. I have the freedom to live in the present and build abundance

1784. I enjoy every presence towards making my dream come through

1785. I am kind-hearted

1786. I am at peace over every situation

1787. I am saved, the past is gone and channel my energy to the present

1788. My personality exudes confidence.

1789. I am bold and outspoken

1790. I am well mannered

1791. I am healthy

1792. I heal myself of any frustration and anxiety

1793. I have integrity, and I am reliable

1794. I am calm and peaceful

1795. All my deeds, thoughts are filled with love and kindness

1796. I am alive and aware of everything happening around me

1797. I am filled with the infinite power of possibilities and happiness

1798. I am always open to learning

1799. I am the master of my own existence

1800. I exude grace

1801. I am greatly endowed with life

1802. I get better with each passing day

1803. I have faith in my ability

1804. My world is filled with beauty and love

1805. I am determined to put all my efforts towards achieving dreams

1806. I am a creator of peace in my heart and in my soul

1807. I overcome every obstacle with ease and awareness

1808. I become greater and greater with each passing day

1809. I am a force of creation

1810. I am a unique blend of love and power

1811. I am a force to reckon with

1812. I am encouraged by my little wins, and it is possible to achieve greater wins

1813. I constantly learn from my mistakes

1814. My needs are met effortlessly

1815. I am loving my life right now

1816. I am aware of faults, and I work towards getting better

1817. I am special in my own being, I accept my uniqueness, and I am in no competition with anyone

1818. I am a wonderful, wise and beautiful person

1819. The past is gone, and I enjoy every moment of the present

1820. I create my own reality

1821. I am completely open to any change in my life that will help me achieve my dreams

1822. My future is bright

1823. I am in total control of my mind and my feelings

1824. I am deserving of love

1825. I am deserving of happiness

1826. I am deserving of the honor

1827. I am deserving of respect

1828. I am filled with optimizing

1829. I am filled with balance

1830. I am charming

1831. I am gracious

1832. I am marvelous

1833. I am radiant

1834. I am a creative and innovative human being

1835. I am happy in this process of achieving my goals

1836. My mind is brilliant

1837. My soul is at peace

1838. I am brewing with energy and overflowing with joy

1839. I am talented, and I use this gift every single day

1840. I am a loving human being

1841. I am guided in everything that I do by courage, love and kindness

1842. I am brave

1843. Creative energy surges through me and leads me into brilliant ideas

1844. I am happy with the blessings I have been given

1845. I am blessed with unlimited potentials to succeed in life

1846. I am aware of my habits, and I can constantly work to improve on them

1847. I am admired

1848. I acknowledge my own self worth

1849. I am a powerhouse

1850. I am indestructible

1851. I am confident that every bad thing would pass and I will be blessed with the valuable lessons

1852. My future is an ideal projection of what I envision now

1853. My obstacles are moving out of my way

1854. My path is carved towards greatness

1855. I am powerful at heart, and I have clarity in my mind

1856. I am at peace with everything and everyone coming my way

1857. My nature is divine, I am a spiritual being

1858. My life is just beginning

1859. I am excellent in everything that I do

1860. I use my full potentials, and I yield good result

1861. My mind is filled with only positive thoughts, and these thoughts are the ones creating my future

1862. I am in the process of positive change

1863. I am divinely guided and protected at all times

1864. I claim my power and move beyond all limitations

1865. I trust the process of life

1866. I am deeply fulfilled by all that I do

1867. I prosper everywhere I turn

1868. I am in inspiration for others

1869. I am a good listener

1870. I am trusted by people

1871. I accept my past, and I get over it

1872. All things work together for my good

1873. I am surrounded by wonderful people

1874. I am balanced both mentally and physically

1875. I devote a portion of my time to helping others

1876. The world is blessed because I am in it

1877. I am a blessing to this world

1878. I am pain-free and totally in sync with life

1879. I know that old negative patterns no longer limits me

1880. I am willing to ask for help when I need it

1881. I am involved only in healthy relationships

1882. I am always treated well

1883. I don't have to prove myself to anyone

1884. I come from the loving space of my heart, and I know that love opens all doors

1885. I walk in new ideas

1886. I am in harmony with nature

1887. I am safe in the universe, and life loves and supports me

1888. Nothing can irritate or annoy me, I choose to be at peace

1889. I experience love wherever I go

1890. I am willing to change for the better

1891. I am clean from negative thoughts and habits

1892. I choose to see clearly with the eyes of wealth

1893. I cross all bridges with joy and ease

1894. I accept my wrongs, and I learn from them

1895. I keep my distance from all drama

1896. I balance life between work, rest and play

1897. Negativity is a stranger to my life

1898. I act as if I already have what I want

1899. I release all destructive criticism

1900. I love life

1901. My income is constantly increasing

1902. My healing is already in the process

1903. I am constantly willing to learn, there is always room for more

1904. I now live in limit love, life and joy

1905. I become more lovable every day

1906. I deserve all that is good

1907. I am constantly improving my health

1908. Love is my golden rule

1909. I accept that which I cannot control

1910. I am love

1911. I was made with divine intentions

1912. I am adventurous

1913. I feed my spirit, I train my body, I focus my mind

1914. It is my time for greatness

1915. I am my own superhero

1916. I always choose happiness

1917. I will not compare myself with others

1918. I create the change I want

1919. I am chosen

1920. I deserve the best, and I accept the best now

1921. My actions are in complete alignment with my words

1922. I take pleasure in my own solitude

1923. I am a gift to this world

1924. I matter

1925. I am well educated

1926. I am patient

1927. Wonderful things unfold before me

1928. I am intelligent

1929. I am a fighter, I refuse to give up!

1930. I am valuable

1931. I am enough

1932. I am worth living this life

1933. I control my thoughts and the direction that I choose

1934. I create my world

1935. I am more beautiful, and I shine brighter every day

1936. I am proud of the person I am becoming

1937. I honor my strength and my gifts

1938. I am in love with the way I feel

1939. I trust my inner voice always

1940. I give the best part of me to the world

1941. I offer the world my gifts and talent

1942. I begin right now to move towards my life's purpose and goals

1943. I deserve good people around

1944. I decide what my life's purpose is

1945. I am relaxed within me regardless of any challenges

1946. I create and enjoy peace in every situation

1947. I feel my whole being with the light of love, peace and happiness

1948. I breathe in peace and breathe out fears

1949. My mission is to be a better person today

1950. I am ready for a relationship filled with love

1951. All my connections are significant, and they fill me up

1952. The universe gives back love to me as I share love with others

1953. Everybody that I meet is worthy of my love

1954. I free myself from fear and today I welcome real love

1955. My relationship is filled with love and respect

1956. I allow myself to be loved

1957. I am strong and healthy

1958. I am opened to the free and natural flow of wellbeing

1959. Abundant health and well-being is my birthright

1960. Today I am grateful for the opportunity of balancing my mind, body and soul

1961. I am awakened to receive the highest wisdom

1962. My inner voice guides in every moment of my life

1963. My thinking is clear, organized and focused

1964. I am always aware of the right actions to help me reach my goals

1965. Today I am fully in tune with my inner wisdom

1966. My body is in harmony with my soul and my spirit

1967. I am always open to divine guidance

1968. I am filled with light, love and peace

1969. I treat myself always with compassion and respect

1970. I am not perfect, I am just myself, and I love myself

Master Key Series (Prosperity)

1971. I am proud of myself, and I will be better

1972. I create my own experiences

1973. I am great for all my makes me unique; my traits, talents, and gifts

1974. I am a powerful spiritual being

1975. I can attract everything that I need

1976. I am a spiritual being with beautiful physical experiences

1977. I am at peace with the world surrounding me, and the world is at peace within

1978. I have everything I need to be happy

1979. I give up old beliefs, and I absorb new and healthier ones

1980. I am a positive and important person in this world

1981. I give up old negative thoughts and feelings about me

1982. I am proud of what I have become

1983. I unconditionally love and accept myself

1984. I am unique and special

1985. My life is lovely, everything is well now and always

1986. I live fully and breathe freely

1987. My future is bright

1988. I live now in love, light and unlimited happiness

1989. Every situation will turn out well, and I am saved

1990. All is good in my world

1991. I free myself from any feeling doubt

1992. I accept myself and create peace in my mind and my heart

1993. I am at peace

1994. I am tolerant with myself and with others

1995. I am beautiful and loved by everybody

1996. I am in the process of positive change

1997. I carefully listen to my body's messages, and I yield to them

1998. I am content

1999. I am ready to change for the better

2000. I am grateful for what I have right now

www.ingramcontent.com/pod-product-compliance
Lightning Source LLC
Chambersburg PA
CBHW030659220526
45463CB00005B/1844